The Book of
Dulverton, Brushford,
Bury & Exebridge

Dulverton & District Civic Society

HALSGROVE

First published in Great Britain in 2002
Revised and reprinted 2012

British Library Cataloguing-in-Publication Data
A CIP record for this title is available from the British Library

ISBN 978 0 85704 178 4

HALSGROVE
Halsgrove House,
Ryelands Business Park,
Bagley Road, Wellington, Somerset TA21 9PZ
Tel: 01823 653777   Fax: 01823 216796
email: sales@halsgrove.com

Part of the Halsgrove group of companies
Information on all Halsgrove titles is available at: www.halsgrove.com

Printed and bound in China by Everbest Printing Ltd

*Whilst every care has been taken to ensure the accuracy of the
information contained in this book, the publisher disclaims responsibility
for any mistakes which may have been inadvertently included.*

Frontispiece photograph: *Round-up of the Anchor Exmoor Ponies, led by Sid Westcott, 1973.*

FOREWORD

Having been born in Dulverton in 1943, I feel very privileged to be writing this foreword. During my life in Dulverton as a baker, a fireman and a town councillor, I have seen and experienced many changes in the town. Although Dulverton has retained various different businesses, it now relies more heavily than ever on tourism. Being in the Exmoor National Park has made Dulverton even more attractive to visitors, despite the Earl of Oxford being 'disenchanted' with the land in 1539!

To me, Dulverton and the surrounding area is a unique community in which to live and work. This book honours the people of Dulverton, Brushford, Bury and Exebridge from early times to the present day. I hope that readers will enjoy the history and characters represented on these pages.

MIKE BALSOM
DULVERTON, 2002

Dulverton Bridge, showing an early view of Pound Walk.

Dulverton Church of England School, 1936/37, Garden Class. Left to right (those known): C. Matthews,
G. Summers, K. Chilcott, E. Kennedy, C. Burton, J. Herniman, E. Dale, D. Bale, B. Kennedy, B. Lugg,
D. Gunter, H. Stark, L. Venn, J. Heetly, Bert Cockram, D. Winzer, G. Crocker.

Dulverton enjoying itself during celebrations for the Jubilee of George V or the Coronation of George VI.

CONTENTS

Northmoor Road, Dulverton, before 1905.

The Mount, Dulverton, showing Rose Cottage in the centre and Horner Cottage above on the right, some time before 1911.

ACKNOWLEDGEMENTS

The project of compiling this volume was undertaken by the Dulverton and District Civic Society, with Brenda Massie and Chris Nelder leading a small dedicated team of helpers from the Heritage Centre – an enterprise which involved a vast number of man and woman hours! Brenda Massie has been the major contributor, with other articles being written by Barry Hibbitt, David Hunt, Father Robert Miller, Chris Nelder, John Organ and John Smith.

We have received enormous help in the compilation of this book in the form of photographs, other items and memories being lent by the people of Dulverton and the surrounding area, and by many others who have taken an interest in the project. We have taken great care to record names and dates as accurately as possible, and apologise in advance for any errors and omissions which may have occurred.

Thanks are due (in no particular order) to: Mr and Mrs Sydenham, Mr and Mrs M. Cottrell, Mrs Joan Coles, Mrs K. Nelder, Mr John Organ, Mrs E. Robinson, Mr A. Bawden, Mrs Joyce Colivet, Mr and Mrs Hancox, Revd G. Carpenter, Mr Barry Carpenter, Mr John Atkins, Mrs Joan Garnish, Mr D. Hill, Mrs E. Sandiford, Mrs J. Luke, Mr Allan Ferris, Mr M. Hawkins, Mrs Jean Campbell, Mrs M. Rawle, Mrs S. Martinez, Mr J. Bodger, Mrs Logan, Miss L. Westcott, Mrs E. Baker, The Exmoor Society, Mr Bert Cockram, Mr and Mrs Blackmore, Mrs Doreen Ridler, Mr Hawkins (of Bristol), Mrs C. Adams, Mrs V. Gynn, Mrs Anne Logan, Mr and Mrs Poat, Mr A. Steer, Station Officer Stanbury of Dulverton Fire Station, PC Colin Haddrell, Mr S. Thompson, Father Robert Miller, Mr and Mrs J. Burton, Mr David Hunt, Secretary of the Congregational Chapel and Abbeyfield, Mrs Bricknell, Mrs Isobel Jones, Mr Ian Baird, Revd and Mrs A. Appleby, Mr D. Bales, Mrs M. Stoneham, Mrs L. Sandison, Mr Keith Ross, Mr J. Thorne, Bury, Mrs C. Thomas, Revd and Mrs Flack, Lenton Photographics, Mrs G. Somerskill, Mr John Symes, Mrs Bell, Mrs G. Sinclair, Mrs Mary Baker, Mr and Mrs M. Balsom, Mrs Ellen Maund, Mrs Mollie Leadbetter, Mr C.D. Williams (British Legion), the *West Somerset Free Press*, Steve Guscott, the *Western Daily Press* and *Poetry Now* (Peterborough).

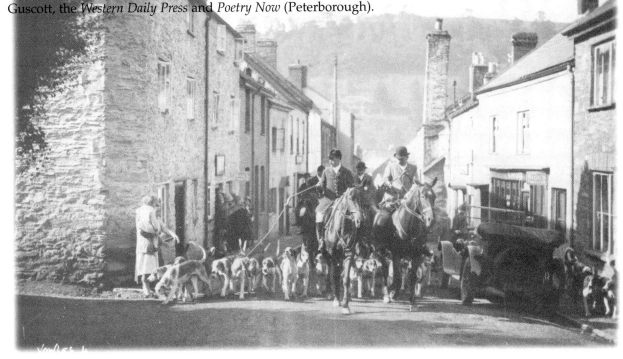

Dulverton town charter, 1556

ONE

❧◈❧

THE TOWN & ITS CHARTER

One could say like Topsy, Dulverton just 'growed', but that is not entirely true. It has in fact taken nearly 2,500 years for it to reach the point it is at in 2002. The earliest known details concerning Dulverton date from the late Iron Age, by which time tracks from the hill both sides of the valley led down to the river, where there was no doubt a means of crossing, perhaps a ford. The Barle – the name given to the river means 'Hill Stream' in Old English – has always been a fast-flowing, slightly dangerous river. Above the river and dominating the Dulverton Valley, is an Iron-Age enclosure, Oldberry; one and a half kilometres upriver is a second enclosure, Mounsey. Iron smelting took place within an area stretching from Oldberry to Mounsey, from the Iron Age through to the fourteenth century, creating a useful industry for the region and ingots for bartering. It seems almost certain that this was the beginning of Dulverton. The river side, once cleared of trees, created an area for a settlement and for agriculture; it remained by or near the bridge right up to the 1300s.

By this time, the church had been built (in the late Norman period) and a very flourishing market took place in front of and around it. There were no barriers; the only road through was the High Street. Barlynch Priory – established in 1160 – was only a short distance away on the Little Exe. Here resided a few of the Black Canons of the Augustinian Order, linked to Taunton and with headquarters at Winchester. They must have been a familiar sight in Dulverton, hunting – with the King's permission – through Dulverton woods. It must be remembered that Dulverton, and its deer, were the property of the King.

From Iron-Age times to the present day, trading has taken place in the area, particularly in Dulverton itself. As agriculture and husbandry improved, so livestock and by-products were traded, with Dulverton gradually becoming the centre of this activity. Wool, leather and iron were the main products when the first charter was granted in 1278. Barlynch Priory had by this time been established for over 100 years. In 1279, Dulverton was declared outside the pale of the Forest by Edward I, although it

was still owned by the King. The second charter in 1306 not only established a market every Thursday, but gave a three-day fair for the Feast of All Saints.

Dulverton had by now at least 12 guilds and a Guildhall for keeping the stamps, weights and measures necessary for trading. It must have been a fairly substantial and secure place, though not necessarily large or ornate. It was where deputy bailiffs and constables met with other parish officers, such as the ale-taster, and the searcher and sealer of leather. Here also tolls, fines, stallage and suchlike were kept by the constable until taken to the lord of the manor.

The Black Death in the 1340s halved the population of Dulverton and its surrounding area. This was also the period when iron smelting ceased along the Barle Valley. From this time on, by accident rather than design, Dulverton and its area (the hundred) fell into the hands of the Prior of Taunton (the Priory being a sub-house of the Abbey of Winchester), for which King Edward III fined him five marks gold and three years rent at £10 per year. Needless to say, all of this did nothing to help Dulverton in any way during an era which was punctuated by endless disruptive events, from the 100 Years War, the Peasants' Revolt and the rise and fall of various kings, all demanding allegiance, men and money. As Winchester was the seat of kings – and the Abbey either for or against that king – Dulverton became, for a period of 150 years, much the worse for wear. In order to make amends and, with encouragement from the Canons of Barlynch, the then Prior of Taunton applied to Henry VII for a fresh and amended charter. This he granted with weekly markets, two three-day fairs and a pied poudre court for the first time.

By now the area boasted spinners and weavers, with fulling mills, grist mills and tanneries. These thriving conditions prevailed until the Dissolution of the Monasteries in 1539 when, once again, Dulverton and its area took a nose-dive in prosperity, having lost the support and drive of the Black Canons. The king was once again responsible for the area and very quickly gave it to the Earl of Oxford who – having discovered more of its position – requested an exchange for other lands. 'Disenchanted' was the term used!

Town Hall, Dulverton.

PROGRAMME

CONCERT and
MINSTREL
SHOW.

Saturday, May 27th.
At 8 p.m. (1944)

PROCEEDS IN AID OF
⚜ SALUTE THE SOLDIER WEEK ⚜

Above: Town Hall, 1927/28. Front: Mrs Horne on the right, with Polly Hawkins.

Far left: Town Hall Programme 'Concert and Minstrel Show', 1944.

Right: Cinema in the Town Hall. The Programme for February 1948 included My Son, My Son *with a coloured cartoon;* The Grand Escapade *and* Death in High Hells; Sioux City Sue *and* Traffic in Crime; Within these Walls *and* The Fighting Lady; Penitentiary *and supporting programme;* Nine Men *and* Painted Boats; God's Country *and* School for Danger; The Wane Case *and* Death Rides the Range.

THE
B.B.
CINEMA
Proprietor — J. H. Blackhurst
DULVERTON

Twice Weekly
Tuesday
and
Friday
One Performance at 7-15 p.m.
(Doors open at 6-45 p.m.)

FEBRUARY, 1948

Price 1d.   Proceeds to:
The British Legion Benevolent Fund.

Left: Town Hall opening of the steps.

By 1553, the beginning of Mary Tudor's reign, the Manor had reverted back to the Crown. In 1555, John Sydenham of Combe applied for a charter on behalf of the people of Dulverton, which was granted, with William Babbington becoming Lord of the Manor. Queen Mary had allowed Babbington, who was a Gentleman of the Privy Chamber, to purchase the Manor for £1,230.5s.0d. prior to 1555 – he already held lands at Timberscombe. With the change of monarchy in 1558, Babbington sold up and Sydenham bought the Manor and hundred. By this time, within the Manor, there were 750 people, 120 dwellings, gardens, 6 dovecots, 6 mills, 30 orchards and 2,900 acres of land.

Babbington appears to have kept the Charter, as application for a copy was made some 200 years later, but only a translation was allowed. Curiously enough, the original 1555 version later resurfaced in 1935/6 in the study of a lawyer, and from thence was returned to Dulverton. One wonders what might have happened after the Monmouth Rebellion when James II demanded the return of all charters in Somerset, Devon and Dorset. Some were revoked, while others were returned with improvements to conditions. Ours was just missing – no wonder we were keen to know what was on it!

THE TOWN HALL

In 1760, it was agreed that a Market House would be built in place of the tottering Shambles, although, in fact, it was another 100 years before the Shambles was demolished. The lower part of the Market House was open and used mainly for market stalls, although at one point in its history it housed the Dulverton fire engine. The upper floor had a room which was used for many functions, including that of a Magistrates Court. The bell tower, called Market Turret, could be seen for some distance around.

The building was in constant need of repair and so, in 1865, a new building was planned and subscriptions were raised. After much debate, the foundation stone was laid in 1866. Efforts were made to acquire the land to the rear, so that the new building could be erected in a straight line. This land was owned by a Mr Kingdom who withdrew his consent to the sale. Whilst this rebuilding was taking place, the Trustees conveyed their thanks for being permitted to use the Boardroom of the Workhouse as a Magistrates Court.

This new Market Hall now had iron gates across each arch, with padlocks. The Trustees agreed that the upper room could be rented out for ten shillings per night. Apart from being the Magistrates Court for some 40 years, the rooms in the upper part of the Town Hall began to be used for various other functions, both social and educational. In 1871, these ranged from a lecture on teetotalism, to a Polytechnic Exhibition and Servants' Ball. A soup kitchen was started to help those affected by the hard times prevailing in agriculture and industry – the rental for which was £1 per annum. By 1873, theatricals were

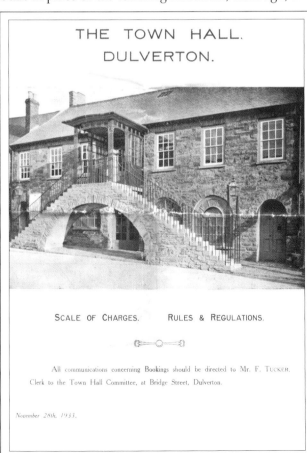

Dulverton Bridges

Barle Bridge, Exe Bridge, Hele Bridge and Chilly Bridge were all built in medieval times and have all been widened since to take traffic. Clockwise from top: View of Dulverton taken from The Cottage – by the time this photo was taken, the Pound had crossed the River Barle from east to west and Mr King's new house was being built next to the Pound; the River Barle at Dulverton, taken from the Doctor's Bridge (which no longer exists) in the early 1900s; Hele Bridge over the Little Exe; Dulverton Bridge before 1895. In the left-hand corner the Old Causeway and ford used to cross the river before the bridge was widened in the early 1800s.

A ticket to a Police Ball held in 1946 and the Police Ball held in Town Hall, thought to have been in the late '50s.

also held, but the upper chamber was used in many ways as it is today for events, lectures, club dinners, concerts and balls. In 1896, an item in the *Free Press* read: 'Dancing was kept up to the early hours to the strains of Mr J. Bale's string band by 100 guests at the annual servants' ball held at Dulverton Town Hall.'

In 1883 Wildman Circus came to town and only paid 6s. (30 pence) for the use of the hall. William Huxtable was appointed as the Town Crier and Superintendent of the Market Seals, Market and Fairs. There was considerable competition between the town's businesses for the best spot to sell their goods by the Magistrates' stairs – a spot usually won by Thomas Catford.

In 1888, under the Justices Steps or staircase, the first urinal was erected – the continuing use of which eventually led to the outside stairs being built in 1927. Also in 1888, the Trustees proposed selling four Chippendale chairs for £1 each and buying new chairs at a cost of £12. In 1894, a witness box and dock were erected for the Magistrates Court and alterations were made to the Stage and Justices Bench. The Trustees decided to charge the Parish Council 2s.6d. for each meeting, which included fires and lights. The Parish Council – perhaps in retaliation – wanted power to appoint more members to the Trustees. There were already two Parish Council members among the Ten Good Men, but the existing Trustees were opposed to any further appointments from that direction.

During the wars, various fund-raising functions were held and the American soldiers built the projection room for the cinema.

Recently, between 1999 and 2000, the Town Hall has enjoyed extensive renovations including a small lift, new kitchen and a smart, welcoming entrance hall.

HMS *DULVERTON*

The first ship to carry the name *Dulverton* was built in 1904 by Richardson, Duck & Co, Stockton-on-Tees, for the Dulverton Steamship Co. Ltd, owned by W.J. Tatem & Co. In April 1907 it sailed for Antwerp from Bahia Blanco with a cargo of wheat – and disappeared!

Dulverton Flood, Barle Bridge, aerial view, 1952.

Clearing the snow, 1947.

DULVERTON FLOOD, 1952

Before 1952 there is no mention of any severe flooding in Dulverton, but the flood of August 1952 – which swept away so much of Lynmouth – caused utter devastation in Dulverton, and is still remembered vividly. For many years it had been the habit of Dulverton men and boys to meet on the bridge and keep a watch on the rising river. This was only done if the rain had been persistent and heavy, with the wind driving off The Chains and the river obviously rising fast. When the river is in full flow, the bridge can be felt to shake. This happened in 1952 when Jack Arnold and his friend were standing on the bridge. Suddenly they saw what appeared to be a wall of trees topped by water coming from Exmoor House. It was horrific! 'Run Jack!' said his friend, and they could run – both being tall, lean men. But by the time they reached Chapel Street, the water had caught up with them. Fortunately they managed to get to safety. Jim Bodger, Dulverton born and bred, was aged 24 at the time. In 1993 he recalled:

On the Friday it had been drizzly – not heavy rain. Coming out of the Town Hall film show there was thunder and lightning. The street lights were still on at midnight. After I thought that was peculiar but the police had perhaps asked them to, because they had fore-warning the flood was coming. Father [was] woken at 5.00am by the Manager of Fishers Builders, saying half of Dulverton had gone and could he come and help. He woke me and said something terrible's happened. I went down about 6.00. There was water crossing the road between the Bridge Inn and the garage. Ray Rendall and I caught a trout crossing the river. I was recruited in as I worked for Fishers. The Milk Bar people made a hole in their roof and crawled through to Mrs Cleeve's. John Stanbury, the Fire Chief at the time, went with a rope tied round his waist, played out from the electricity place, to see if the two Miss Chanters were all right in their thatched cottage in the Old Forge. Three men were tied together and tried to get down Chapel Street, but couldn't do it. There were carrots found in the trees by the bridge, probably from the allotments near Exmoor House. Fred Wilson and I found a beehive in the middle of the street.

They said the clocks at the Boot Inn and the Bridge Inn stopped at 11.45pm although there had been no sign of flooding at 10.30pm when we came out of the film show and walked over the bridge. The Dulverton Fire Brigade was already out at Exford and couldn't get back to Dulverton. The first fire engine came from Chilly Bridge. We were lucky to have no fatalities as they had at Lynmouth. I thought I heard the wind in the trees, but there didn't seem to be any wind and then of course it was the water coming down.

The *West Somerset Free Press* edition of 23 August 1952 was entirely devoted to the disaster and, in pictures and words, showed the havoc wreaked by the flood. It spoke of 'devastation everywhere'; 'the milk bar washed away'; 'the bridge congested with debris'; 'the large garage almost denuded'; 'the damage to furniture and furnishings'; and 'an antique dealer's serious losses'. It told how the services moved swiftly, and of the escape through the roof of Mr and Mrs Watts (the manager of the garage and his wife), who had been marooned in their bungalow.

Derek Bales, who is now a frequent visitor to Dulverton, was doing his National Service with the Army at the time, and was based at a camp near Yeovil. In a letter to the Heritage Centre in the 1990s, he told how they were all roused from bed to help with the flood-relief work:

We left Yeovil at 3a.m. and arrived at Brushford around 5.30a.m. The next two weeks were spent camped in tents in a meadow opposite the Carnarvon Arms – now a small housing estate. During this time we virtually worked from daylight to dark, always in the Dulverton area. After an early morning meal we left camp, and generally were not fed again until our return around 8pm. I remember once being so hungry I called in a village shop, bought a loaf of bread and a 1lb pot of jam, sneaked away for some 15 minutes and ate the lot. I know we spent some time at Tarr Steps clearing the river of trees and other debris, and returning massive boulders to the river bed.

The 6 September edition of the *Free Press* was headed 'Getting straighter'. It spoke of 'Banana distribution in the Dulverton rural area' – an event which, in a Britain still in the throes of post-war rationing, must have been quite something!

Since the flood barrier was created, there has still been periodic flooding, although on nothing like the same scale. The most recent example was in 2001.

In the past, when winters were winters and the River Barle froze, people could even skate on it.

❧ The River Barle at Dulverton, Somerset ❧
by the late Joanna Hearth

The River Barle flows fast in spate,
rushing, rumbustious, roaring, irate,
testy and turbulent past the town,
boiling, boisterous, brutal, brown.

The River Barle is full of spite,
murky and menacing – monitored at night,
grumbling and tumbling so near the edge –
frenzied, frustrated, at the old stone bridge.

And on, 'twixt man made curbs and checks,
merging with malice with the swollen Exe.
Suddenly surging in senseless haste,
they flooded together and laid all to waste.

by kind permission of Poetry Now, Peterborough

✍ Wild Weather ✍

Main image: *Fore Street, 1977, in the snow.*

Above left: *Northmoor Road, 1977, after opening the road.*

Above: *Snow clearing in 1977 – Fred Hawkins leaning on his shovel to the left.*

Left: *Marsh Bridge, flooded.*

Below left: *The Barle, pretending the flood barriers aren't there, 2000.*

Below: *Mrs May Hancox standing at flooded Marsh Bridge, 1999/2000.*

DULVERTON CHARACTERS

An early 'character' was the Revd J.B. Philby, vicar of All Saints from 1892 to 1909. He was somewhat eccentric and had the habit of walking into the church – even for a service – with corn seed in his pockets, muttering 'I'm going to feed my birds' and offering the seed to the eagle on the lectern. In 1903, in an article entitled 'An Unexpected Episode', the local paper referred to a 'Presentation at Dulverton Town Hall', in connection with the Scripture Union and the Young Women's Bible Class. It was attended by local dignitaries including Lady Gwendoline Herbert, Lady Margaret Herbert and Dr Collyns, who presided. After Dr Collyns' opening remarks, the meeting was addressed by the Dowager Countess of Portsmouth, who presented prizes to children for giving correct answers during Bible study. She was thanked by Lady Margaret Herbert and the presentation was made, with thanks and further speeches. The report continues:

It was now about 8.30, and the programme was not completed, when the Vicar rose from his place in the body of the hall. He said he agreed with what Lady Portsmouth had said. But she had made an important omission. She had not mentioned Jesus in her address. The rev. gentleman, concluded his speech thus: 'Christ is the Head of the Church; the Church is the head of the Bible, and I am the Vicar.' He then walked to the platform and asked if he might close the meeting. Lady Portsmouth, motioning to Dr Collyns, said: 'I think it would be advisable, don't you?' The Vicar pronounced the Benediction and left the room. The audience then dispersed.

The premature termination of the meeting has since been the subject of a good deal of comment... the unfinished part of the programme comprised some more singing and thanks to the Chairman.

Arthur 'Farmer' Chilcott had a few cows and fed them on the grass growing on the road verges. He could never keep off the cider and was known to emerge from the Lion Tap and attempt to ride his cycle up and down the steps of the Town Hall – to the accompaniment of the rattle of bottles in the front basket! As a result of the cider, he was frequently rather fuddled, which made the timing of his milk round somewhat erratic. He brought around two churns of milk, one suspended on each end of a shoulder 'yoke' while his customers brought out their jugs to be filled via Arthur's pint measure.

Arthur was a regular churchgoer, and his rich bass voice could be heard reciting a psalm or two on his rounds. At Evensong his voice boomed across the church, irritating one lady worshipper so much that she wrote a letter of complaint to the Bishop of Bath and Wells. 'We cannot hear ourselves sing, with Mr Chilcott sitting behind us.' The Bishop, it seems, tactfully suggested she should move to another pew.

Arthur was a great mimic of Sir Winston Churchill. In 1940, when the war was going badly for the Allies, he was in the Lion Tap one night, imbibing too freely of his favourite tipple. For some reason, and in his best Churchillian voice, he announced: 'the whole of the Atlantic Fleet has been sunk.' A passer-by heard it and thought it was the wireless and that it must be authentic! Like lightning, word spread around the district – and much further afield – no doubt causing great consternation, until it was contradicted.

Alec Passmore was quite a different character. He was a highly skilled poacher, specialising in salmon. It was a constant battle of wits with the water bailiff. So it was that Alec had a special pair of trousers made, so formed as to allow a salmon to be suspended from his waist. This led to a rather peculiar gait, but no matter; he could pass the bailiff, with no salmon visible. He also made a good living catching trout, rabbits and pheasants – one just had to order them. Just after the end of the Second World War, he caught 125 rabbits in one night and sold them for five shillings each. However, he shared a liking for cider with his great friend Arthur, and this could have had tragic consequences. At about 2.00am one winter's night, a carpet of snow adding to the cold, two people hurrying home noticed a white mound in the Recreation Ground. Bending down, they noticed it was Alec, completely 'cidered up' and legless. Somehow, between them, they got Alec home.

John Ford was a gentleman's hairdresser or – as he would say – 'Tonsorial Artist'. Haircuts in the town were not just haircuts – they were an event. There was always laughter coming from the barber's shop which sported in the window a big ear, a huge comb and a pair of sheep shears. One holiday-maker had John cut his hair with the old hand sheep shears, so that he could go home and tell his friends. The shop was also used as a refuge by some locals; as women didn't usually go into barbers' shops the men could have some peace and quiet. On one occasion, while John was cutting a visitor's hair, one of the locals said quietly (but just loud enough for the customer to hear): 'you'll never be able to put that right John, you've cut too big a piece out.' John, who could see by the look on the visitor's face that he'd heard, turned to the local saying, 'keep quiet, he won't notice.' When it came to show him the back of his hair in the mirror, John showed only the left side. The customer craned his neck to see the damage and asked to be shown the other side. When it turned out to be all in order, he realised the joke, thanked them all for an enjoyable morning and said he looked forward to his next visit. Another customer was told that the spray he'd chosen for his hair was used for killing woodworm!

Sadly, John had to retire owing to ill health in 1976, with the loss to many Dulverton men of a great deal of innocent entertainment.

The High Street, looking towards The Cottage, c.1880. Some properties still have thatched roofs.

Main: *High Street (Back Street) before modernisation.*
Inset: *Hangman's Alley.*

TWO

HOUSES, ESTATES & FAMILIES

Prior to the mid-nineteenth century, Dulverton streets and alleys had different names to those we know today. The Shambles occupied the centre of what is now Fore Street, with King Street on the Town Hall side and Queen Street opposite, running from the Copper Kettle to the corner where Dulverton Fruit and Vegetable Shop is today. Market Street ran from the Copper Kettle to Lady Street; what is now Bank Square was called Broad Street.

The entrance to Lady Street was so narrow that a cart could not pass through, so, in 1840, the Town Trustees paid £30 to have the end of the house opposite the Post Office taken down. Union Street was on the other side of the road and much narrower. There was no entrance to the churchyard from Broad Street at that time; the space was occupied by private property. Church Lane was known as Princes Street, which was, and still is, a privately-owned cobbled way.

The Fry family at Old Shute Farm. Left to right: Edgar, John, Polly, Lizzie.

The only way to church – except for the path called Church Steps which runs from Catford Lane, ending in a stile between the cottage and the church – was the little path that still exists from Lady Street. In 1855, the Trustees spent £48 on the church wall, thus improving the churchyard and its approaches.

At the lower end of the town, what was known as Duck Paddle is now called Chapel Lane. Duck Paddle led into Mill Ham Way and Throgmorton Street, which passed the laundry to Sealeys. Across Mill Ham Way was a toll-gate and toll cottage near the present Congregation Church. Throughout this small town, there were little alleys and passageways such as Rosemary Lane, which led to fields, gardens and orchards. Cabbage Lane was between the White Hart and Bastille House.

In a survey carried out for the manor of Dulverton in 1554 on behalf of the lord of the manor, a cottage at the east end of Barle Bridge was occupied by John Pearse and was one of the few buildings named. Gradually, over the next 100 years, this little cobbled street evolved and lead down to The Pound and the lime pit. It is also known that at this time there were a few 'shops'. Unfortunately, all the buildings in this area of the town were destroyed by fire in 1917.

Leading from Bridge Street into High Street, the big building on the far left of the photograph *(page 18 top)* is called Governor's House, built in the early 1700s, replacing two small houses. The bucket in the foreground may have been used for 'dipping water' from the gutter. The leat or one of the town's pumps was the only means of getting a water supply.

On the left of this photograph *(page 18, bottom, main)* is Middle House, in the centre of which is one of Dulverton's secret places known as Hangman's Alley *(page 18, inset)*. Looking further on is the Lamb Hotel (which has been renovated recently into flats). Continuing up the High Street, in the 1980s, you might have seen a llama parked outside what was then the pet shop – now further along the road. Round the corner into Jury Road, you will see some of the oldest thatched buildings in Dulverton.

The Cottage, on the other side of the river, has been a landmark since the early 1800s. It was built along what was, at that time, the only and oldest road into and out of Dulverton on that side of the river. It was built for the Fry family of chocolate fame. Rumour has it that the cottage – often mistaken for a Tudor building – was pictured on the lids of chocolate boxes. To the west along the hill – hidden for much of the year by trees – is a much older building known as **The Mount**. Down the hill are **Horner** and **Rose Cottages** and a handful of others.

Also of note is **Pixton Park,** which has been home to several prominent families, such as Dyke Acland and that of Lord Carnarvon (including Herbert and also Sydenham) as at various times all inter-married.

Main: *Pixton Park front entrance before 1895.*

Far left: *The rear entrance before 1895.*

Left: *Pixton House.*

Main: *The 1st Somerset County Show ever was held on the field below Pixton.*
Inset: *New Bridge, Dulverton – crossing the Barle from Station Road to Pixton, before 1980.*

Above: *Hollam House, from a postcard of 1921.*

Right: *Staff at Hollam House, 1908 – an official photograph. Standing 4th from the left is Annie Sedgbeer; Sidney Passmore is the groom.*

Left: *Hollam House staff, 18 August 1908, including some of the outdoor staff.*
Left to right, back: *Harry Copp, Ethel Connett, Tom Chamberlain, Annie Sedgbeer, ? Lake, Winifred Thomas, Walter Steer, Sidney Passmore; seated: Dora Passmore, Milly Bond, Germaine Caper.*

Above: *Barons Down House – used by prisoners of war – now demolished.*

Left: *'Below-stairs' staff at Barons Down House, before 1900.*

Below: *Barons Down senior household staff, before 1900.*

Mowing the lawns at Barons Down.

Hollam House, once the site of a Saxon holding, has been preceded by many different buildings and has been owned by several different families including the Sydenhams, Beagues and Mildmays, who continued through until the mid 1980s. The renowned Letitia Shoppee was born a Mildmay and lived at Hollam for much of her time. Part of the Hollam Estate was **North Combe Farm** where, from 1800–1908, the Catford family were tenants. George's son James was apprenticed in 1807, and James' son George in 1841. Hyla – many of whose photographs are included in this publication – was a professional photographer and organist at All Saints.

Out of Dulverton on Bury Hill was **Barons Down House**. The Lodge could be seen on the Minehead Toll Road. **New Invention Cottage** – part of the North-moor Estate created by John Locke above Marsh Bridge – was later owned by Sir Frederick Wills (elevated to the peerage as Lord Dulverton).

The Peppin family have been a part of Dulverton for many generations – at least since 1600 – and intermarried with the Sydenham family. Elizabeth Sydenham married Humphrey Peppin, whose son, also Humphrey, obtained permission for his mother and his half-brother to bear Arms and Crest. This was obtained from the Earl Marshal of England – Edward, Duke of Norfolk. The family was also noted for developing the breed of Merino sheep in Australia. Although basically landowners, they had other irons in the fire and many properties including **Old Shute**.

Combe belonged to the Reigny family from before the fourteenth century to the late-fifteenth century. In 1482, it passed to the Sydenham family, when Edward Sydenham married Jane Combe, and remained with that family until 1872, when the estate was sold to Tom Doddington.

The Carpenters of **Gulland** represented a rural artisan class who, at various times, were tenant

G. Catford, North Combe Farm, early 1900s.

Indenture of James Catford dated 30 September 1807 – son of George Catford of Dulverton, who was apprenticed to Richard Pine of Oakford, tailor.

Left: *Woodleigh Chimneys, one of the oldest dwellings in Dulverton.*

Below: *Woodleigh and Garden before 1900. Mrs Pearse with her daughters Ellen (Mrs G. Catford) and Mary (Mrs Snell); the child is Monty Pearse, son of Hector.*

Below: *Cottages which were later destroyed by fire (1917). Stanbury's repair shop, which leads to the veterinary practice, now stands on the site.*

Bottom: *Looking down Fore Street, c.1900.*

New Invention Cottage, early 1940s.
The photograph was taken by an evacuee.

Left to right, above: *The late Lord Dulverton, 1970s; Walter and Emma Williams, parents of Leonora Mary 'Polly' Hawkins; Carpenter Family – Gilbert Carpenter, Philip Carpenter, his wife Priscilla (née Vinson) with Rebecca on her knee, Edgar by her side, and Priscilla sitting in the basket chair.*

The llama kept at Gulland Farm, whose owner often walked with it into Dulverton so that it could carry the shopping home.

Combe House, 1950.

farmers, rural business owners or skilled tradesmen. The following is taken from Priscilla Carpenter's *Common Place Book*:

The summer of 1903 was very wet and a lot of hay was spoilt; some was not cut at all. Corn sowing was very late and catching the corn harvest was difficult. A tremendous lot was spoilt and hundreds of acres ended up not being carried. I've had five acres spoilt, the rest was saved fairly well. I hear a great quantity is now being ploughed down. It is heart-aching to hear of the distress. I carried in January, being 42 shillings the ton. I've bought £4 worth to save our stock. We finished corn harvest on 11 November. Potatoes are scarce and dear, from 8 to 10 shillings per bag.

May 1904
It is a nice growing time. Apple blossom is looking

splendid. Corn in many places is a great failure, it seems to die away. People think it is owing to the wet harvest of last year. We have very poor broods of geese, only ten out of thirty eggs have hatched. I saved mine until they were a good size and then the cats killed four and injured another one very much. Chickens are very good so far. Ducks are selling well – 6 to 7 shillings per couple, while chickens are 5 to 6 shillings per couple.

A Dulverton "At Home"

25

Above and right: *The Cottage, Dulverton.*

Below left: *Label to Mr Abbot re. delivery of game to The Cottage.*

Below right: *Estimate from German Bros for painting the outside of The Cottage, 9 May 1905.*

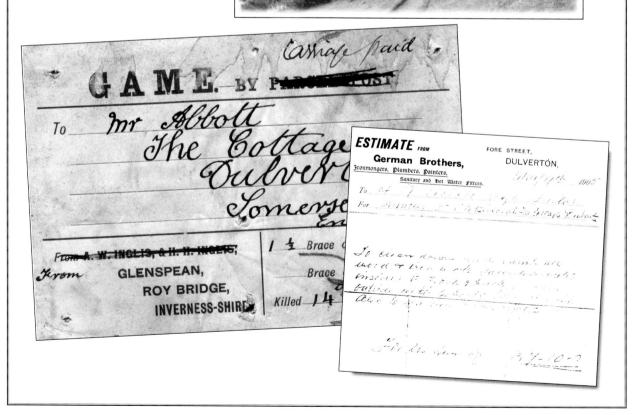

THREE

❦❧❦

DULVERTON AT WORK

Over the centuries Dulverton has had many and varied businesses. Constant change has enlivened the town and given it its unique identity. There have been spinners and weavers, fullers, tanners, harness and saddle makers, boot- and shoemakers, tailors and dressmakers, hatters, not forgetting printers and photographers and – the staple of West-Country towns – butchers, bakers, chandlers, blacksmiths, wheelwrights, wagon and coffin makers. All of these have come and gone – some are still here, creating the hub of Dulverton and its district.

At the centre of this hub were the weekly markets and twice-yearly fairs with traders coming in from far afield, bringing gossip and news and foreign goods – keeping the local shopkeepers and traders on their toes and creating prosperity. However, in the late 1800s, Lord Carnarvon, the then lord of the manor, decided the cattle part of the market would be better sited at the Carnarvon Arms and railway station, thus bringing a greater change. Not to be outdone, the people and traders decided they could benefit from the railway and its passengers and set about creating places within their homes for people to stay, upgrading and rebuilding – changing the face of Dulverton. Even guidebooks were written.

Dulverton Laundry was one such enterprise. It started life as a grist mill and was recorded in 1784 as part of St Barbe, Sydenham's Estate. This continued until the enterprising Mr Palfreyman purchased it from the owner and spent a considerable sum of money converting it into a woollen factory. Thus Dulverton entered the Industrial Age, using the water from the leat to provide power for making heavy-duty cloth and blankets. As the demand for these items lessened the mill went from producing woollen cloth to crêpe material, employing upwards of 70 workers. Around 1840, the mill was weaving silk and making lace. This, however, did not last for more than a few years as imports from Europe were cheaper than could be produced here. This led to another change of use for the building. A wood joiner's factory was set up, making windows and doors needed for the new properties being built in the area, and this is how the Puttock family came to own the building, Peter and his son Arthur being carpenters by trade. Mrs Arthur Puttock set up a laundry, to make use of the remaining buildings. All the water used came from the leat. Eventually, in 1935, Rodney Peake and his sister Maria acquired the laundry and totally modernised it, setting up a dry-cleaning business, eventually to expand right across Exmoor. The vans are still a very familiar sight today.

According to records dating back to the early-seventeenth century, Forge Cottage in Bridge Street was a smithy and wheelwright's from the time it was built, more than 400 years ago. The last blacksmith to live and work there was William Chanter. On 31 May in 1652, an inquest was held in Dulverton into the death of James Hill. Many witnesses declared him to be 'a sick and broken man' when he came to the blacksmith's shop to have some work done. He suddenly fell sick at about 9.00 in the morning and was taken into the blacksmith's house, where he died at 8.00 that evening. The witnesses who took oaths on

Laundry staff, 1980.

Left: *Mackneys frontage, 1951.*

Below: *Thorne Outfitters frontage; the closing sale, 1951.*

Below left: *Greenslade Cycle Shop, Back Street, early 1920s.*

Bottom left: *Woods Café and bakery, advertising homemade cakes, 'no factory ones'.*

Bottom right: *National Provincial Bank staff, 1937. Left to right: Don Garnish, Ken Oliver, Frank Pearce, A.J. Couch, John Bennett.*

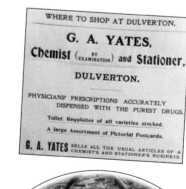

this solemn occasion were: Will Lyddon, John Joyce, Amyas Towte, Abraham Bryant, Edward Addycott, Nicholas Hayes, Will Raymonte, John Coomer, Nichademas Wood, John Farthing, John Lee, Will Bickham and James Brown Ford – women being noticeably absent! Over the next few centuries, there were other blacksmiths and forges in the town.

On the corner of Bridge Street, close to Forge Cottage, was Holland House, built as a private residence over the leat some time in the early 1700s. It had many owners and many uses in the twentieth century, including the Electricity Shop. Opposite Holland House was A.J. Court, in a building and shop which was previously Moore & Stimpson, a tailor and outfitter for the owners and staff of the large estates and, at the time of writing, a second-hand and antiquarian book shop, Rothwell & Dunworth.

There are two large garage businesses in the town, one of which was started by Walter Ridler with a single taxi in a small workshop in Jury Road. The business was expanded by moving into coaching and haulage – with the help of Walter's sons John and David – and is now run by grandson Gary, who joined the firm in 1986. It is a very successful national and international coach business, together with the garage, filling station and MOT-testing station. The earliest known Stanbury Garage was on the corner of Fore Street and Union Street and it was demolished in the late 1970s. The present garage has its repair shop on the corner of Barle Bridge and the car-sales showroom is on Vicarage Hill.

With the advent of the supermarket in modern times, many residents forget that until about the 1970s, all meat and meat products could only be purchased from the local butcher's shop. Dulverton gave great choice to the customer and the competition must have provided a considerable challenge to the local butchers. As recently as the mid 1950s, there were no less than four butcher's shops operating in the town: Mark Goodland on the corner of Union Street and High Street, in the premises owned (in 2002) by Webbers Estate Agents; Oliver Windsor, in Fore Street, subsequently owned and operated by Gordon Summers and, at the time of writing, owned by Gerald David; Maurice Summers who traded from premises on the corner of Fore Street and High Street, later converted to provide the hardware store and fish-and-chip/take-away shop; and a small shop at the rear of the Bridge Inn at the entrance to The Castle, owned by Bill Land, and later owned and operated by his son, Peter.

Two of the butchers owned their own slaughterhouses; that of Oliver Windsor was to the rear of his shop – moved in Gordon Summers' day to the end of Guildhall Terrace – and Maurice Summers' in premises at Millhams Lane. There was once a third slaughterhouse at Barnsclose, opposite Barnsclose Farm. Legislation requiring improved standards saw the Guildhall and Millhams Lane slaughterhouses

close between 1974 and 1985. In 2002, Gerald David is the only remaining butcher's shop in Dulverton and he has a slaughterhouse in Porlock.

Banks opened up in Dulverton in the last gasp of the nineteenth century. In 1898, the National Provincial Bank of England Ltd purchased from Arthur Charles Locke of Dulverton the dwelling house, stables, courtlage and gardens – called collectively Buckingham House and Coltards – for the sum of £1,000. The bank was built alongside the house to form the corner of Bank Square and is little changed from what we see today. The house – now solicitors' offices – became the bank manager's home. The garden is still intact.

Greenslades in High Street was an early example of a combined business. It dealt in and repaired bicycles, car spares and repairs and – in the early heady days of motoring – would fill a car or can with petrol from a hand pump, attached to the wall by the shop window. The mind boggles as to where the tank of petrol was stored!

George Barrell was just one of Dulverton's shoe- and bootmakers and repairers. He bought his shop from Lock the saddler in the early 1920s, certainly before 1926. George was born in Saxmundham, Suffolk, in 1897. He was posted to Somerset during the First World War and came to love it. After his discharge from the Army, he came and set up shop here in Dulverton. He was a regular churchgoer and bell-ringer for many years and, during the Second World War, served as a Special Constable until 1946. He met his wife Ada Combe in the Lamb Hotel and they married in 1950. In 1954 George retired and sold his shop and machinery to Frank Pooley, who continued to trade until he also retired.

Just across the road from Barrell's, forming the junction with the High Street and Fore Street, is a building known as The White Hart – a mid- to late-sixteenth-century building – which served as an inn and was of some importance in its heyday. By the twentieth century, various trades and businesses were being carried on in parts of the building and two other small buildings had been attached, like leeches, to it. After the 1952 flood, Miss Dashwood – whose first Milk Bar venture at the Barle Bridge had been destroyed – set up shop in The White Hart, calling it the Golden Guernsey Milk Bar and serving the most delicious meals and cream teas ever imagined. The milk and cream came from her own herd of Guernsey cows and all the food was homemade, baked on the premises. This continued until the 1960s. This delightful old building must have felt much as it did in earlier times.

There were several small dairies selling and delivering milk in and around Dulverton, all with their own hamlets or small areas. One of the best known was Fishers Dairy in Lady Street. Every day, twice a day, their cows would come through Dulverton from the pastures to the milking parlour

❧ Dulverton Butchers ❧

WHERE TO SHOP AT DULVERTON.

Established Half a Century.

FRANK GOODLAND,

BUTCHER,

HIGH STREET,

DULVERTON.

Above: *T. Uppington,
butcher – he is the man
in the bowler hat.*

Left: *Goodlands
Butchers – Mark
Goodland, wearing an
apron, is standing
outside the shop on
the corner of what is
now Webber's Estate
Agents.*

Right: *Exmoor Meat
– at the time of writ-
ing, Webbers Estate
Agents. This view is
taken looking along
Union Street towards
the Post Office, before
the wall and garage
to the left were pulled
down.*

Barlynch Priory ruins and Barlynch Farmhouse, home of John Venn, born 1832.

and out again. As soon as they appeared, shop doors would be shut, as it was not unknown for a cow to wander in and around a shop as the owners, mouths clamped tight, held their breath! Fishers were perhaps the first to bottle their milk for easy delivery and anything in size from a quart to a third of a pint. This went on until the mid 1970s.

As in most towns, there were several bakeries, but unfortunately only Woods Café, later Balsoms, near the bank survived into the fifties. Balsoms made the best lardy cake in the West Country. The bakery and café is still there (no longer Balsoms, but trading under that name) and still producing excellent bread.

In the late 1800s, Thorne Bros, drapers and outfitters, took on and extended the premises of Ocock (sub-postmaster, chemist and general trader) next to the Lamb Hotel. Thorne's had their head office in Tiverton and remained trading here until 1951, when they sold the business to Tom and Nora Mackney. They operated for several years but, by the 1970s, business had declined and in 1975 they sold out. By this time, Jean Ford had opened her small wool business. Jean really joined her husband John who was a gents' hairdresser and barber who, in 1959, had re-opened a former barber's shop owned by Ron Duncan. Jean and her wool were tucked under the stairs, so to speak.

Barlynch Quarry was owned at one time by Dulverton Rural District Council and was positioned near the ruins of the old Priory, on the original toll-road to Minehead which had been built in 1835/40. The quarry and Dulverton Rural District Council were frequent customers of W. Chanter, the black-smith at Forge Cottage, as were the Exe Valley Electricity Co. Ltd and many others including perhaps the best-known local business, German Bros, ironmongers.

The Germans were a very large family who owned the corner of Dulverton that contained their shop and stores (today the Library, Visitors' Centre and the Heritage Centre), and also several cottages in Dulverton. One of the German family was the very

good and frequently copied professional photographer, J.H. German. In the 1890s, John Hill German (J.H.), with help from Will and Lewis German, purchased 'Pike's', a two-up-two-down cottage, with yard and stone-built shed, butting up to the church-yard. (Pike's had been known as Escurials.) Here, J.H. set up his studio. He converted the shed where he stored all the chemicals and plates, adding an upper floor for dark room, drying room and studio for photographic and portraiture, which was becoming fashionable in the late-nineteenth century. By 1895, this converted shed was extended to the old barn and milking parlour owned by G. Fisher of Fisher's Dairies. J.H. German lived and worked at Pikes until 1913, when he and his wife and children went to Paignton.

By 1981, the present owner of 'Pikes' had acquired the cow shed and yard that had formed part of the dairy and, in the process of repairs, found two pieces of stone. Put together they formed a tombstone with the following inscription – the exact date and age of which could not be determined:

Here
Lies the Body
of EDMUND VALENTINE
of this Town, Felmonger,
Departed this life March...1767
Aged...6 years.

Was this an acquisition from the demolition of the old church in the 1850s?

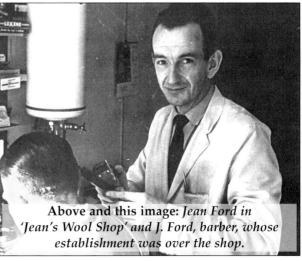

Above and this image: *Jean Ford in 'Jean's Wool Shop' and J. Ford, barber, whose establishment was over the shop.*

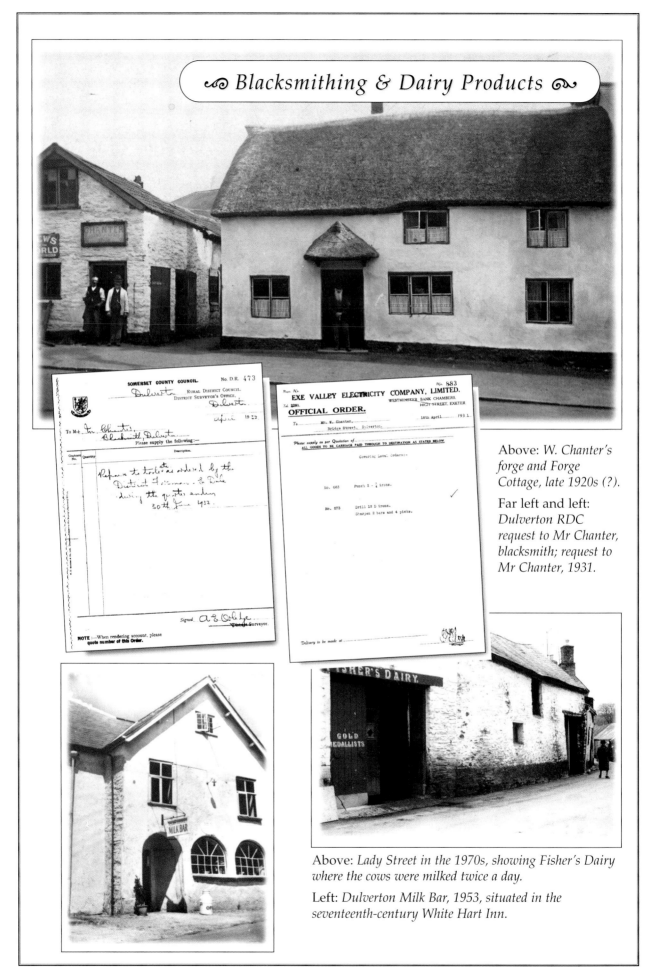

❧ Blacksmithing & Dairy Products ❧

Above: *W. Chanter's forge and Forge Cottage, late 1920s (?).*

Far left and left: *Dulverton RDC request to Mr Chanter, blacksmith; request to Mr Chanter, 1931.*

Above: *Lady Street in the 1970s, showing Fisher's Dairy where the cows were milked twice a day.*

Left: *Dulverton Milk Bar, 1953, situated in the seventeenth-century White Hart Inn.*

҉ Garages ҉

Left: *W. Ridler's first garage and filling station, 1951/52.*

Below: *Walter Ridler in late 1940s with his taxi – Walter started the business with his taxi and a small workshop shortly after the war.*

Left: *J. Ridler & Sons' fleet of coaches and yard, Jury Road.*

Far left: *In 1985 the garage was enlarged with lock-ups and office.*

Above, centre left: *Installation of new petrol tanks and the rebuilding of the garage.*

Right: *Barle Bridge and Stanbury's garage.*

❧ *Holland House* ❧

Far left: *Holland House, 1939. The cows are on their way to the milking parlour in Lady Street.*

Left: *Letter to Miss Dobbs of Holland House from the Dulverton Electric Light Co., 1927.*

Below left: *Bill to Miss Venn, Holland House, 1932.*

Below: *Bill to Miss Dobbs, Holland House, 1932.*

Bottom: *Holland House dressed for the coronation, 1953. At the time of writing the building houses Anthony Sampson Antiques.*

FOUR

❦

DULVERTON AT PLAY

The people of Dulverton have always known how to enjoy themselves. On 17 April 1897, they were given the vote on what to spend their money on. The votes were as follows:

> *A meeting of Dulverton inhabitants discussed schemes to celebrate Her Majesty's long reign.*
>
> | | |
> |---|---|
> | *Paying off the debt on the Town Hall* | *9 votes* |
> | *Widening Lady Street* | *4 votes* |
> | *Provision of public seats* | *16 votes* |
> | *Provision of recreation ground* | *39 votes* |
>
> *Favourite option was: 'feasting and general rejoicing'.*

Nothing changes! When offered the choice between several options to celebrate and mark Queen Elizabeth II's Golden Jubilee in 2002, the result was virtually the same. For a period of four days, Dulverton was lit up and waving flags.

Major national events such as jubilees, coronations, festivals and victory celebrations have always been marked by a beacon at Courtdown. The Annual Carnival has replaced the three-day Fair of our Charter of All Saints. In his day, Arthur Chilcott – a well-known local character whose exploits are recounted in another chapter – acted as auctioneer at the auction which always followed the Carnival. Produce collected from farmers all over the district was brought together at the Lych Gate – apples, plums, pears, turnips, cabbages and so forth, all the proceeds going to charity. The Carnival has continued to be popular. In October 1955, the *Free Press* reported:

> *Crowds invaded Dulverton for the town's 47th carnival. The turnout of walking masqueraders was the poorest for 30 years, but there were excellent tableaux. Stephanie Harris was carnival queen, and Vivienne Lang and June Phillips were princesses.*

From around 1900, there has always been a race down the Barle, finishing at Dulverton, in aid of local charities. The earliest record we have is from 1903 when a group of young men – organised by The Lion – raised funds for charity by racing each other down the river. In the past there were also raft races, but these too have given way in recent years to the duck races, possibly because the water companies are now authorised to take water from the Barle and there is insufficient flow in the summer to keep the rafts afloat.

DULVERTON SILVER BAND

This is from Edgar German's memories of the band:

> *I don't know when the band was started, but I know that my grandfather William German used to play in it in the 1880s. Later my father and my uncle played in it and I started practising in 1911... I was about eight and a half years old and I was on the Cornet... When World War One started, the band folded up but we soon got it going with us young ones joining the old regulars. We would play at sports and fêtes and at Christmas, as well as playing out in the streets.*

He goes on to tell how the band decided to get a good bandmaster and approached Fred Loosemore, who was returning to Somerset from Canada where his band had won the Canadian Championship. Two Dulverton men agreed to pay his fees and, having listened to the band play, Fred said, 'I think the best way is to start with scales.' Fred continues:

> *I think all our hearts went down in our boots. I know mine did... we thought we were a good band. We soon found out that Fred Loosemore thought we had a lot to learn – we were sloppy, not cutting off notes, not holding on to notes and so on... he wanted 'More bass!' I was the only bass player and had to make up my volume to suit. After every practice my gums were bleeding... four years later I had to have all my teeth out!*

After three years, during which time some band members gave up, they began to play in public again. 'I believe we really shook Dulverton,' recalled Edgar. 'They had never heard anything so good before and huge crowds used to turn out to listen to us.'

As their instruments got older, Fred decided they must have new ones. Edgar remembers:

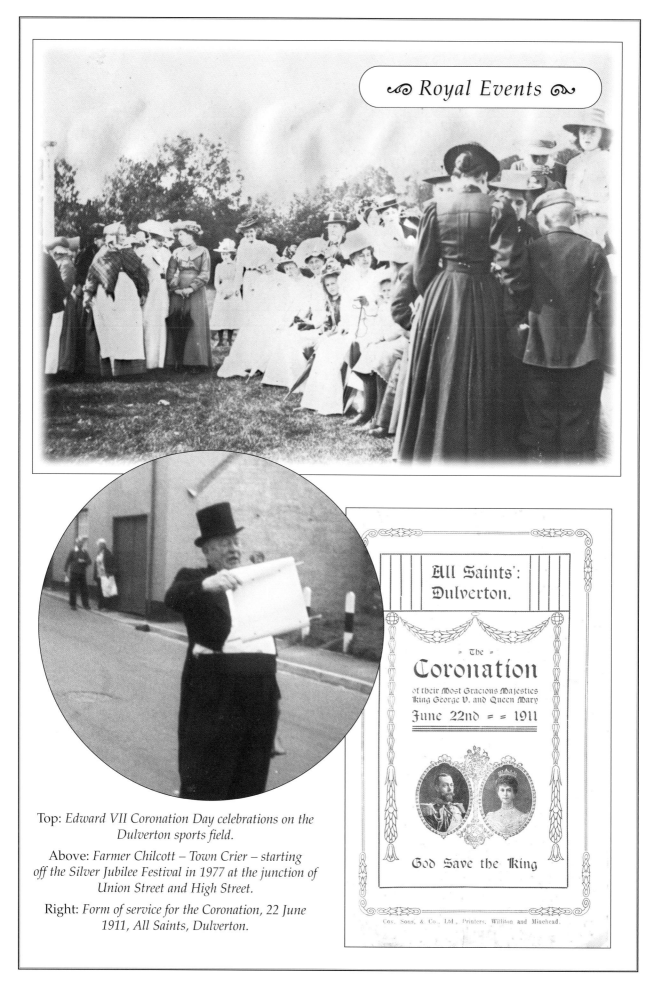

Royal Events

All Saints': Dulverton.

The Coronation

of their Most Gracious Majesties King George V. and Queen Mary

June 22nd = = 1911

God Save the King

Cox, Sons, & Co., Ltd., Printers, Williton and Minehead.

Top: *Edward VII Coronation Day celebrations on the Dulverton sports field.*

Above: *Farmer Chilcott – Town Crier – starting off the Silver Jubilee Festival in 1977 at the junction of Union Street and High Street.*

Right: *Form of service for the Coronation, 22 June 1911, All Saints, Dulverton.*

Arthur ('Farmer') Chilcott and Capt. Bill Liley (proprietor of the Lamb Hotel) at the Donkey Derby, 19 July 1966. 'Farmer' was Dulverton's last Town Crier.

We arranged a jumble sale in Marsh Hall and we were so popular by then that it must have been the jumble sale to end all jumble sales. Lorry after lorry load of it, not only jumble but good stuff as well... we made enough to buy a set of silver plated instruments... today it would cost £20,000 to set up a band. So that was how Dulverton Brass Band became Dulverton Silver Band.

Another jumble sale the following year produced uniforms with each member paying for his own trousers. The band went to Cardiff for the National British Legion Rally, to be attended and inspected by the Prince of Wales at Cardiff Castle:

There must have been at least a 100,000 legionaries there and about 100 or more bands. The Prince of Wales came round and inspected us. When he got to our lot he asked Capt. Popkiss where we came from and, on hearing his reply, said 'Oh, I know Dulverton very well'... After the inspection we were off... The Prince and Earl Jellicoe were on the top step taking the March Past. Just before we got there, a man from the Prince of Wales' staff detached himself and came straight out in front of us. He then guided us around the statue until we were facing the marchers, in line with the Prince of Wales and 20 feet away from him... we realised that he had picked us out of all that lot to play at the saluting base! A month or so after that we heard we had been on the newsreels in the cinemas.

By this time the band was playing every fortnight in the street, at sports meetings and carnivals and the annual band concert in the Town Hall was always crowded. Edgar remembered an incident in which the band was involved:

Dulverton Carnival was famous... we used to get thousands of people here. Fireworks would be let off in Fore Street outside the ironmongers and were the most popular part... we had a very good display. Around 1933, a Sergeant Bull had come to Dulverton and had stopped the fireworks. The sergeant started walking up the street to go to the Police Station and then it seemed as if the whole crowd had turned into an angry mob. Soon he was being pelted with eggs, a lot of them bad

and smelling strongly. The noise was getting louder by the minute so Fred picked out a piece he thought might calm it down. As soon as we started, they started fitting words to the music, all against the policeman. We changed the tune and the same thing happened again. 'We're only making it worse,' said Fred, so we stopped playing, but the shouting was worse than ever. A lot of the eggs missed Sergeant Bull, but the bandsmen had their fair share. Some of them were plastered from head to foot. By this time they were shouting 'Let's get him down the river. Throw him over the bridge.' ... my uncle Fred and Bert Page got down round the back to head them off saying 'If you go on like this, you will kill him. We are taking him home.' ... and so they did, even though the mob was still shouting and trying to get at him.

The following year the fireworks were held in the sports field and Sergeant Bull was moved elsewhere. Edgar also remembers that:

Another honour accorded to the band was at the end of the Second World War. The BBC sent down a recording van to record us as part of the national celebrations that were to go out in the evening on the radio at ten o'clock... That's how we came to start the national celebrations which ended with a band in Trafalgar Square.

A combination of circumstances brought about the ending of the Silver Band. A law was introduced to say that only organised charities could collect money, which meant the band lost much of its income. That, and the advent of pop music, took its toll and the band folded. How we wish we had had it for our next celebration!

Christmas Party for the laundry in the Retreat, now a Youth Hostel. Left to right: Mrs Herbert, Mrs Sloley and Mollie Elston.

Left: *First Dulverton Carnival Queen, 1940s (?) – all garments were made of crêpe paper.*

Below: *Carnival float, 1956/57.*
Left to right, fairies: *? Gunney, Lizanne Radley, Daphne Sommerwell, Sheila Gunney, Jane Sharp and Marianne Rawle.*

Below left: *Carnival float, 1955 with Carnival Queen, Stephanie Harris, aged nine, being crowned by Mrs Campbell-Morgan.*

THE
WISHING WELL

JUNIOR

N⁰ 25

PRICE 6D.

Dulverton & District

Fortieth Grand Annual

CARNIVAL

In Aid of TAUNTON, TIVERTON and
MINEHEAD HOSPITALS, EXETER EYE
INFIRMARY, DULVERTON and DISTRICT
NURSING FUND and THE EXETER
ORTHOPAEDIC HOSPITAL.

PROGRAMME

...be given
...lding the
...gramme
...St., Dulverton.

DANCING

at the

Town Hall

on Saturdays

Sept. 7th, 14th, 21st, and 28th.

Oct. 5th, 12th, 19th and 26th.

Thursdays

Sept. 12th and 19th.

Oct. 10th, 17th, 24th and 31st.

THE EXMOOR DANCE BAND,

REFRESHMENTS.

A grand Boxing Tournament

held in UNION HAM (by kind permission), on Sept. 14th.

Commencing at 7-30   Promoter...Mr. W. SYDENHAM.

Judges...Mr F. SMITH (Tiverton) and Mr. A RANKIN (Dulverton).

Referee...Lt-Col. O. G. B. PHILBY.

Timekeepers...Messrs. RON GERMAN and BEN CORNELL.

3 Round Contest—
R. HAWKINS (Tiverton) v. KEN NEWMAN (Plymouth)

4 Round Contest—
FRED ROWE (Tiverton) v. TOMMY HILL (Plymouth)
(A.C.F.S. Champion. & Finalist National Cadet Champion 1945)

4 Round Contest—
L. KING (Tiverton) v. D. Penny (Plymouth)
(S.W. Area Champion S.C.F. 1946)

3 Round Contest—
E. TOOZE (Tiverton) v. R. RUNDAL (Plymouth)

3 Round Contest—
COTTREL (Plymouth) v. R. PARSONS (Plymouth)

3 Round Contest—
S. CRIDDLE (Tiverton) v. LEN CHAPMAN (Minehead)

Special Attraction—DON HOOLE of Plymouth.
Trained by Tommy Price, ex-Feather-weight Champion of England, and under
the management of Jimmy Wilde, ex-Fly-weight Champion of the World

A Grand SIX 3min. Rounds Return Contest

DON HOOLE v. **BILLIE MACK**
(Plymouth)   (WALES)

A coming Champion. Who recently fought Hoole & wants to reverse verdict.
Referee—Mr. PHIL FLETCHER of Tiverton.

Six 3min. Round Contest
KEN HUNNING (Plymouth) v. DUG FOSTER (Redruth)

Four 3min Round Contest
FRED TAYLOR (Plymouth) v. HARRY TIPPET (Newport)

Town Hall,

Dulverton.

Wednesday, Sept. 26th

ARTHUR HAMBLIN

The Flutterbyes

COMEDY CONCERT PARTY

in Two Hours of Mirth & Melody.

The Cast includes :—

MURIEL ALLEN - B.B.C. CONTRALTO
JOHNNY PHEAR - The Singing Accordionist
PEGGY & JUNE - In Song & Dance
STRAVANI - Versatile Violinist
TONY MARSHALL - The Singing Newsboy
JOE WARD - A Concert-in-a-Turn
ARTHUR HAMBLIN COMEDIAN
Late of Happy Valley, Llandudno, Skegness Etc., Etc.

A GRAND SHOW FOR A GRAND CAUSE.

Book Seats Early at Ellertons Stores.

Prices :— 3/6 & 2/6 (reserved) and 1/- (limited)

DOORS OPEN AT 7-30, COMMENCING AT 8 O'CLOCK

Above left:
*Carnival float,
1952.*

Above and left:
*Programme
no.25, 40th
Grand Annual
Carnival.*

∽ Carnival Time ∾

Left: *The Carnival float of 1936 which won first prize.*

Below: *A Carnival float from 13 October 1927 – Bales' lorry.*

Dulverton Carnival Concert

OCTOBER 15th, 1920.

⁜ PROGRAMME. ⁜

SONG	"Just keep marching along"	CHORUS.
SONG	"Ca-bages, Ca-beans and Car-rots"	Mr. UPPINGTON.
SONG	"When poor old father tried to kill the Cock-a-doodle-do"	Mr. CHILCOTT.
VIOLIN SOLO	"Mazurka"	Mrs. DREW.
SONG	"Blackbird Love"	Mrs. C. B. St. JOHN MILDMAY.
SONG	"Tony, the Swiss Mountaineer"	Mr. CLIFFORD ECCLES.
SONG	"That old-fashioned Mother of mine"	Mrs. LITTON.
MONOLOGUE	"Billy"	Miss ETHEL GERMAN.
SONG	"Zummerset Cream and Cyder"	Miss UPPINGTON.
HUMOROUS ITEM	"A Song without a Name"	Mr. WILL FOSTER.
SONG	"Where do flies go in the Winter time?"	Miss F. GERMAN.
SONG	"I know where the flies go!"	Mr. THORNE.
SONG	"A Fairy went a marketing"	Mrs. DREW.

INTERVAL. FIVE MINUTES

CHARACTER MONOLOGUE	"Lasca"	Miss ETHEL GERMAN.
COMEDY DUET	"Pennsylvania"	Messrs. FOSTER & ECCLES.
SONG	"A big lot of sunshine"	Mrs. LITTON.
SONG	"Bertie"	Mr. CHILCOTT.
VIOLIN	"Selection"	Mr. DULLINGHAM.
SONG	"The Garden of Forgetting"	Mrs. C. B. St. JOHN-MILDMAY.
HUMOROUS SKETCH	"A Serial Story"	Mr. WILL FOSTER.
SONG	"Waiting for the Moon To shine"	Miss BROOM.
VIOLIN SOLO	"Gavotte"	Mrs. DREW.
SONG	"Jumpers"	Miss UPPINGTON.
SONG	"I'm on the Staff"	Mr. CLIFFORD ECCLES.

⋯⋯ GOD SAVE THE KING. ⋯⋯

PIANIST : MRS. GAGE.

THIS PROGRAMME IS SUBJECT TO ALTERATION.

Above left: *Carnival concert, 1920.*

Above: *Carnival, 2001 – Kids are Us/Dulverton Child Care Centre – the float depicted Snow White and the Seven Dwarfs. The children are: Witch: Rosalie Tribe; Prince: Adam Cottrell; Huntsman: Toby Cottrell; Snow White: Rachel Stevens; Rabbit: Willow Tribe.*

Left: *A float from 1985.*

Let There be Music!

Dulverton Silver Band with their new uniforms, early 1920s.

Exmoor Dance Band with Stan Ayres on piano at Dulverton Town Hall.

⌒ *Festivals & Fêtes* ⌒

Above: *Ready to join the fête to raise money for Wings for Victory, 1944. Tony Puttock is in the pram.*

Left: *ARC stall, Dulverton Festival, 1987/8, with Nellie Hill and Phyllis Fisher.*

Above: *Festival, 1987. Lorna, played by Rebecca Addicott, is being kidnapped by a Doone, played by Paul Chanter.*

Right: *Coach and four used between Dulverton and Lynton for a Festival.*

Above: *The top of Bridge Street with Holland House on the right, late 1920s. The two elderly people third and fourth from the left are Tom Marley and his wife, licensees of the Boot Inn.*

Right: *The stables at the Lamb Hotel. Charlie Hoskin and a prize-winning mare.*

Below: *The Lamb Hotel.*

FIVE

⌖

PUBS

Dulverton's reputation for having 19 or more pubs is well founded. There were several maltsters and malt-houses. At one time, those who could – and this was most households – made cider and/or brewed light ale, not just for their own use but to sell to others. This certainly proved easy if a presentable 'parlour' with benches was available. Most houses in Dulverton were named and these are among the pubs known until the introduction of licensing laws reduced their number:

PUB	SITE AS AT 2002
The Groom & Porter	location not known
The Anchor	Town Mills Cottage
The Boot	part of N. Western Farm House, Bridge Street
The Ram	became The Lamb Hotel – now a block of flats
The White Hart	Antique shop & Estate Agent
The White Horse	Floribunda and Charity Shop
The Red Lion*	The Lion
The Barnstaple	Webbers Estate Agents
Nightingales	Two houses built on the site
The White Lion	next to Governor House – now The Wardrobe
The Bridge*	a latecomer, built in 1845
The Rock*	converted in the 1800s from a smithy
The New Inn	Doctor's Surgery
Wrens	a small alehouse, but a good maltster which must have served the Country House Inn next door
Country House	Wreneaton now occupies Wrens and Country site
Dolphins	later Buckingham House and the Bank House – probably an Inn in 1700
Green Hotel	Greenways

still in existence today

The Lion took over the Barnstaple Stables (at the time of writing the town car park) which had a name board saying 'Lion Hunting Stables'. It stabled patrons' horses, and also rented out hacks for hunting.

The Lamb Family and Commercial Hotel (Posting House) not only stabled horses, but provided considerable livery for local people as well as visitors. The Lamb Yard was for a very long period under the care of Charlie Hoskins.

An advertisement from 1924.

43

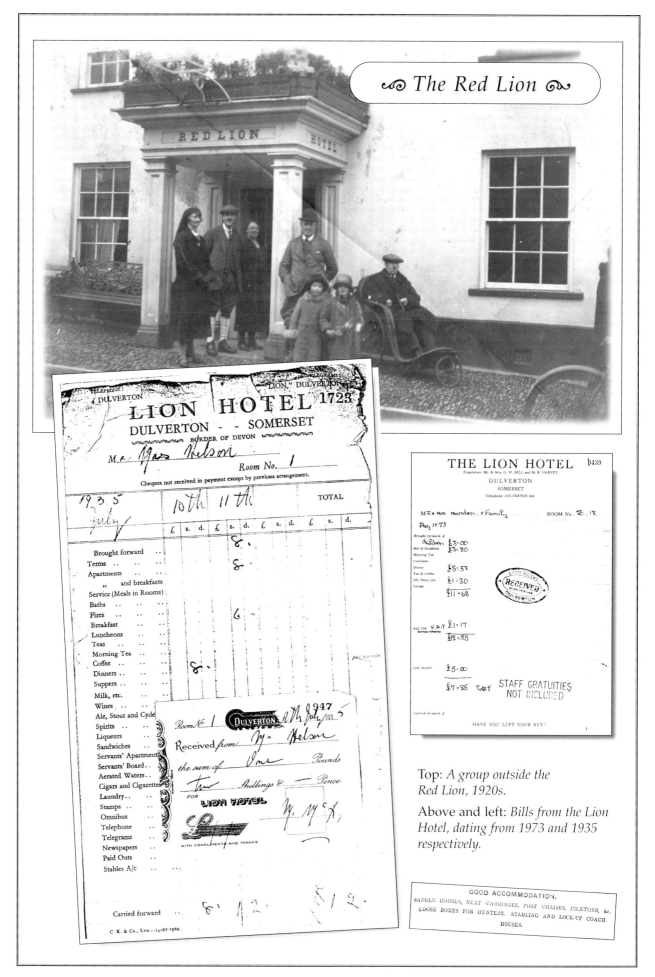

❧ The Red Lion ❧

Top: *A group outside the Red Lion, 1920s.*

Above and left: *Bills from the Lion Hotel, dating from 1973 and 1935 respectively.*

Six

SCHOOL DAYS

The earliest evidence of any formal schooling in Dulverton dates back to 1736, when Elizabeth Dyke and her son Edward of Pixton Park endowed a charity school for 30 poor children in Dulverton. They set up a trust of £12 payment per year from the rents of Leigh Farm in Winsford, then occupied by Edward Smyth. The trust continued until 1923, by which time this charge had been placed upon other property still held by Pixton Park Estates.

It is not recorded how the 30 children were selected or whether those picked regarded it as a pain or a pleasure! The earliest school was held in the church house, but in 1760 this building was demolished and a corn and butter market built in its place, with a schoolroom above.

From the early 1800s until the 1940s, dame schools catered for some Dulverton children, including at least one famous one – Sir George Williams (founder member of the YMCA), who was born near Dulverton at Ashway Farm in 1821 and received his first education at the hands of Mrs Timlett, who kept an old-fashioned dame school in the High Street, before moving on to a grammar school in Tiverton.

Another dame school, run by Mrs Bagg at 2 Church Lane, was known by the grand title of 'Baggs Academy'. A third, 'Wreneaton', at Vicarage Hill, was still in existence in the 1930s. The first national Church-of-England school was built in 1860 up Catford Lane.

For nearly 100 years, Dulverton Top School – later known as Dulverton First School – provided an education for most Dulverton children throughout their school life. However, in 1958 the then Dulverton Secondary Modern School was built for those aged 11 to 16. Mrs Sylvia John (née Herniman), born in 1910, remembers:

I went to what we called the Top School. We had two hills to climb to get there, and my simple mind made me feel I went to a very high school. Our headmaster, Mr George Price, was very, very strict... The children were petrified of him, and we were not very enamoured with his staff! The punishment for boys was to lie across the desks and have a good whacking with the cane! (One of my brothers soon caught on and stuffed his trousers with old newspapers before going to school!) Girls would get a whack with the ruler across the hands and stand 'for eternity' with their nose in the corner. So it's a wonder we learned anything at all, but that school turned out some very brilliant people.

Mrs Mabel Welsley, born in 1908, also recalls her school days: 'I wasn't very happy there. I never used to stay home from school, but I would have done if I could have!'

Charlie Steer, born in 1911, remembers the boot club introduced by Sir Gilbert Wills, later Lord Dulverton, where children paid in a small sum once a month:

Mr George Price's wife used to take the money we brought in... When it came to the summer holidays we used to have to go to Northmoor, and parade in these boots, and the money that we couldn't make up they used to make up for us, so that was one way of getting a new pair of boots.

Jim Bodger recalls the arrival of evacuees in 1939:

I can remember waiting to see the evacuees arrive, wondering what they would be like, and then giving up when it became dark. Dulverton Top School carried on almost as normal with some additions, the evacuated schools using the Parish Rooms, Marsh Hall and Town Hall. One of the teachers from the school using the Parish Rooms, a Mr Fisher, was questioned by the Police about a small attaché case he always carried with him, thinking he might have been a spy. His explanation quite simply was that it was his hearing aid. He was deaf!

Some of the evacuees were taught in the Town Hall, where groups were divided into two, with a teacher at each end. An example of the children's schoolwork came to light recently under the Town Hall floorboards when it was refurbished in 1999. During the war, Mrs Savage and Bobby Cornell put the Town Hall kitchen to use to cook food for the schools.

A former evacuee – a Mr Edwards – called in at Dulverton Heritage Centre in 1999. He told how he

❧ Page one of the Extinguishing Order of the charitable foundation ❧
established by Elizabeth Dyke and her son Edward in 1736 to
provide schooling for 30 poor children in Dulverton.

Sealed 28 September 1923.

No. 23/695 E.

Stamp £1.10.0.

County - SOMERSET.

Parish - DULVERTON.

Foundation - ELIZABETH AND
             EDWARD DYKE.

Order for extinguishing
rent charge.

ORDER made by the Board of Education under the Charitable
Trusts Acts, 1853 to 1894, in the Matter of the Foundation
of ELIZABETH AND EDWARD DYKE, being one of the SCHOOL
CHARITIES, in the Parish of DULVERTON, in the County of
SOMERSET.

THE BOARD OF EDUCATION hereby ORDER as follows:-

The transfer of the sum of £480 Consols made on the 22nd
day of August 1923, being then of the value of £280.16.0 by
George Francis Sydenham, of Dulverton aforesaid, Medical Officer
of Health, into the name of the Official Trustees of Charitable
Funds in trust for the above-mentioned Foundation, shall take
effect and operate as a final and absolute redemption of the
Yearly Payment of £12 formerly charged upon a messuage and
tenement called "Leigh" situate in the Parish of Winsford, but
at present charged or alleged to be charged upon or issuing out
of certain land and premises known as "The Mount", situate in
the Parish of Dulverton, now in the possession or ownership of
the said George Francis Sydenham, and as a complete and effectual
compromise and adjustment of all claims on behalf of the Foundation in respect thereof, and the said Yearly Payment shall
henceforth cease, and be absolutely extinguished, and the Order

Top left: *Annie Gregory with her baby sister and grandmother, c.1874.*

Top right: *Annie – Miss E.A. Gregory, c.1887.*

Above: *Annie and Mr Hawkins on their wedding day, c.1890.*

Left: *Annie's sampler, c.1880.*

Dulverton School 1915/16. Left to right, back row standing: ? Venn, ?, Bessie Hawkins, ?, ?, ?, ?, ?, ? German, ? Milton; middle: *Bessie Bead, Polly Williams (later Hawkins), ? (later Mrs Milton), head teacher, others not known;* front: *first five from left not known, Cliff German (husband of Bet), others not known.*

School gardening class with some of the Bury children and headmaster, Mr Weaver.

Dulverton C- of-E School on Empire Day 1924/25. The head, Charles Weaver, is standing on left by window.

Dulverton School 1924, Group 2. Left to right, back: Frank Adams, Dennis Chilcott, Wilf Milton, Ron Williams, Arthur Lynch, Derry Williams, Jack Kelland; middle: *George Taylor, Charles Steer, Arthur Chilcott, George Bristow, Maurice Puttock, Fred Newton, Ken Billings, Charlie Courteney, Jim Greenslade;* front: *Doris Cottey, Mabel Curtis, Elsie Kendal, Celia Scrivens, Dorothy Hitchcock, Doll Pollard, Louie (?) Broom.*

Dulverton School 1924, Group 3. Left to right, back: *Harry German, Frank Lang, Eric Lambert,*
Lewis Huxtable, Alex Passmore, Fred Lynch, Fred Herniman, ?; 3rd row: *Vera Westcott, Gladys Chanter,*
Margery Steer, Ruth Hobbs, Betty Balsom, Sid Gale, ?; 2nd row: *Flossie Hanford (Bolt), Louise Takle,*
Zilla Tarr, Evelyn Huxtable, Cathy Williams, Elizabeth Saunders, Nelly Lang, Nora Strickland;
front: *Alex Erskin, Jim Kelland, Fred Jones, Felix Rendell, Bill Martin.*

Dulverton School 1924, Group 4. Left to right, back: *Roy Chilcott (killed in the Second World War), ? Takle,*
Clifford Gunter, Maurice Rooks, Jack Broom, Walter Pollard, Ralph Sloman, ? Greenslade;
3rd row: *Ouida Passmore, Marian Chilcott, Vera Westcot, Nora Milton, Elizabeth Starks, Joyce Lambert, Doris Pike;*
2nd row: *Margery Herniman, Pam ?, Nelly Ford, Ivy Gale, Joan Arnold, Joyce Chanter, Mary Herniman, ?;*
front: *Douglas Litton, Lewis Huxtable, Bert Steer, Gilbert Lang.*

Above:
Dulverton Boys XI, 1948/9. Left to right, back: *Ken Norman, Archie Chanter, Joe Liddiment, Bob Coggins, Mervyn How, ? Holden;* front: *Michael Hobbs (?), Gordon Chilcott, John Biggs, Alan Mitchell, Alan Steer.*

Above: *Schoolwork belonging to evacuee Edna Nichols, dating from 1940/1. This was found beneath Dulverton Town Hall during the 1999 renovations.*

Left: *Church Lane, 1940s, showing a boy outside No. 2, once a private school run by Mrs Bagg and known to the youngsters as 'Old Baggs Academy'.*

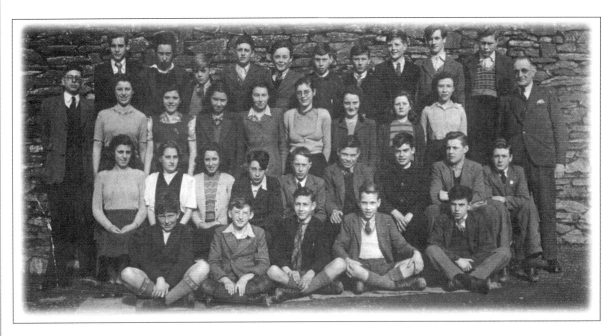

Dulverton School 6th Form, 1950 Autumn Term. Left to right, back: *Gerald How, Gerald Chaplin, Owen Rowcliffe, Clive Heard, Bruce Kemp, Ron Fry, Michael Farmer, Alan Hutter, Dave Smith, Tony Crook;* middle: *6th Form teacher Mr Dennis Elliot, Dorothy Yerbury, Margaret Gigg, Maureen Hunt, Violet Thomas, ? Ellis, Shirley Verron, Mary Mitchell, Amy Judd, Mr Charles Weaver, headmaster;* seated: *Doreen Cridge, Gwen Walker, Daphne Clark, Brian Radley, Pete Andrews, Tony Puttock, Alan Tarr, Alan Steer, Derek Sparks;* front: *Bobby Needs, Mike Gammon, Mike Hobbs, Mervyn Priddle, Fred Chilcott.*

Dulverton Church of England School Football Team, 1951/2. Left to right, back: *Dennis Elliott, Jimmy Adams, John Hobbs, Maurice Judd, David Hill, Albert Harvey, George Mogford, 'Plum' Warner;* front: *? Billings, Jimmy Ellis, Ray Cridge, Ray Farmer, Alan (Pepper) Patterson, Graham Bidgood, Peter Nott.*

Above: *Church-of-England School, 1962.*
Left to right, back: *teacher (name not
known), Brian Woodcock, Steve Petts,
Diane Hutter, Andrew Jones, Ben German,
? Newton, Derek Sparks, Miss Banbury
(teacher);* standing: *Pat Vellacott, Carol
Tarr, Cosmo Fairwell, ?, Elaine Coggins,
?, Peter Jones;* seated: *Diane Foster, Steve
Thomas, Lesley Thomas, Michael Summers,
Alan Ferris, Barry Summers, Janet Rawle,
Phil Takle, Peter Summers, Julie
Nurcombe, Sandra Wilkinson, Christine
Ferris;* front: *Rosie Truelove, Elizabeth
Takle, Denise Wilkinson, John Nurcombe.*

Above: *Dulverton Middle School
Teachers, 1976.* Standing: *John
Broughton-Thompson, Jan Ross, Tony
Longborne, Bill Buscombe, Paul Hague,
Graham ?, Mollie Hudson;* seated:
*Bettye Nelder (Secretary), Linda James,
Douglas Juckes (Headmaster), Nancy
Ross, Freda Bevan, Jean Luke.*

Left: *A Victorian experience at
Dulverton Middle School.*

and his younger brother and sister were billeted first at the Vicarage, then, within a few days, split up, his siblings going to a Mrs Gibbs in Northmoor Road, and he to Mrs Bet German at the Heritage Centre premises, then a cottage. He remembered their arrival in Dulverton:

A large group of unaccompanied children had come by train from Kent 'to get away from the Germans'. Having arrived from Dulverton Station on the local bus, the first thing we saw was 'GERMAN' over the shop. I started to shake, while my sister turned to me in tears saying, 'We are too late. They are already here.'

Dulverton residents also had their first sight of nuns during the war when, in 1940, a Catholic school was evacuated to Hollam House, the home of Letitia Shoppee – a very curious sight for the uninitiated!

Until the Beeching cuts in 1965, a few children attended Tiverton or Taunton Grammar Schools, catching a bus from Dulverton Town Hall to get the train at Dulverton Station, but the vast majority were educated at the Top School.

In 1967, when the three-tier system was introduced in West Somerset, the Top School became known as Dulverton First School, catering for children from the ages of five to nine; the Secondary Modern School became the Middle School for those up to 13, older children now completing their education at the West Somerset School in Minehead.

The First School's magnificent view of Burridge Woods and the town was offset by the difficulties posed by its steep and narrow access, its outside toilets, and the absence of a playing field and other modern facilities. All this resulted eventually in the building of a completely new school, 'All Saints C of E School', which was completed in February 2000 and incorporated the re-housed Nursery Unit. It was officially opened by the Rt Revd A.J. Radford, Bishop of Taunton, on Friday 5 May 2000.

Right: *Dulverton Middle's pool.*

Below main: *Dulverton First School 1860–2000, showing the main school block, with adjoining house. The house was used by successive head teachers as their 'tied accommodation' until the mid 1960s when it was converted to an office, a staff room and the school library. The main school hall and a further classroom were added around 1950. Fire destroyed a classroom in the main building in 1983.*

Inset: *All Saints School, which opened in February 2000.*

SEVEN

಄ৰ৯ৡ৩ঌ

EXMOOR HOUSE

THE WORKHOUSE

Long before the Poor Law Act of 1834, Dulverton Trustees sought to help their very poor and needy. This was done by collecting tolls and stallage on market days and fair days. Some of this money was used for repairs, renewals and necessary wages, but there was always a certain amount of cash left and, come pay-out day, notice was given of the date by the church. This took place in the Barnstaple Inn and later in the Red Lion.

In 1830 the Town Trustees rented – at a peppercorn rent – an empty house in Princes Street (now Church Lane) and this became Dulverton's first poorhouse, with limited accommodation for the very needy. Unfortunately this house caught fire in 1838. Nevertheless, the people of Dulverton preferred not to have a custom-built workhouse and managed to avoid doing so until the powerful County authorities threatened the Dulverton Trustees and Guardians with dire consequences.

Sister Ormash, matron, outside the workhouse, 1937.

So the Trustees and the townspeople put their heads together and concluded that the architect already employed in the rebuilding of their church should be commissioned to design and build the new workhouse. This was Edward Ashworth.

He produced the building one sees today which won considerable acclaim for its good looks and design. But for all this, the local people made considerable efforts never to be put in it! With this in mind, the Dulverton Friendly Society had evolved in 1819 and was very well established by 1856.

It is important to remember that being poor in those days was almost inevitable for people who earned a pittance from their labours, so much so that being a labourer invited destitution. An amendment to the Poor Law in 1834 was introduced to force the regions to build workhouses and to cut back on public relief of the poor – a sort of tax which was greatly resented by the somewhat better-off citizens. The thinking was that if the poor were provided with a bed and food, they would not need to claim relief. The workhouse forced the healthy into a prison-like environment, a place where the happiness of the inmates was of minimal importance.

The Dulverton Guardians consented, under duress, in July 1853 to build the workhouse to house up to 60 people, at a cost not exceeding £1,500. By the end of the year a meadow was bought for £675 and by the following June, a Mr Shadbrook's tender of £2,811 was accepted. The neo-classical-style building – to be known as Exmoor House – was completed to Ashworth's design in 1855. In the autumn of that year, a Mr and Mrs William Hiles responded to an advertisement and were appointed as the first Master and Matron in January 1856. He got £25 per annum and his wife was paid £15 per annum, plus their rations.

It was not a rest-home, for workhouses were made unpleasant, if not brutal in atmosphere, through the imposition of strict discipline. The intention of the amended law was to persuade the poor to better themselves, in addition to removing an unwanted financial burden from the public's neck. Ashworth's building resulted in a deliberately segregated establishment with specific areas for men, women, adults and juveniles. There were ten single beds in the men's bedroom and a dozen double beds in the women's. Every room had a purpose; day rooms, sick room, surgery and laundry, and so on.

Living conditions were very basic and so was food. Meat was a luxury and generally the inmates survived on bread, soup, chicken and rabbit, and anything else edible that they could get their hands

ᥫ᭡ Taunton Union Regulations, 1914 ᥫ᭡

TAUNTON UNION.

Regulations relating to the

BATHING & CLEANSING

OF

CHILDREN AND ADULTS

NOT BEING INMATES OF THE SICK OR LUNATIC WARDS.

WHEREAS by Article 47 of the Poor Law Institutions Order, 1913, the Guardians of the above-named Union are required to make regulations dealing with the above matter.

It is hereby ordered that:

1. Every Inmate shall be bathed on admission to the Workhouse unless the Medical Officer, after the examination prescribed by Article 7, or similar regulations in force within the Union, gives directions to the contrary.

2. Except in cases in which the Medical Officer considers that it is undesirable, every inmate shall be bathed once a month, and shall have the option of being bathed at least as frequently as once a fortnight. Should there be any doubt as to the advisability of bathing any Inmate, reference shall be made to the Medical Officer.

3. In preparing a bath, the cold water must always be placed in the bath before the hot water.

4. Before any Inmate enters the bath the officer in charge of the arrangements shall ascertain by a thermometer, the temperature of the bath, which should be not lower than 80 degrees of Fahrenheit, and not higher than 98 degrees of the same scale.

5. During the bathing of inmates the bath room must not be left without some paid officer or servant appointed by the Guardians and distinctly made responsible for the conduct of the arrangements.

6. Every hot-water tap shall be provided with a key, which should be kept in the permanent charge of an officer of the Workhouse, and may be entrusted temporarily to the person responsible for the bathing, but to no one else. On the termination of the bathing, the key must at once be returned to the officer permanently responsible for its safe custody. The above-named persons should also be responsible for the hot-water taps not being used in their absence.

7. During the bathing of Children the officer appointed must always be present.

8. In the bathing of all classes of inmates the water used shall be changed, and a fresh supply provided for each inmate bathed. In all cases an inmate has the right to demand water which has not been previously used.

9. A separate towel shall be provided for every inmate of every class bathed; and the bath towel must always be washed before being used again.

10. Any marks, bruises, wounds, sores, local pain, or evidence of disease of any kind, complained of by the inmates or noticed by the person in charge of the bathing, shall be at once reported to the Master or Matron, and if necessary, by them to the Medical Officer.

By Order,
W. F. B. DAWE,

4th March, 1914.

Clerk to the Guardians.

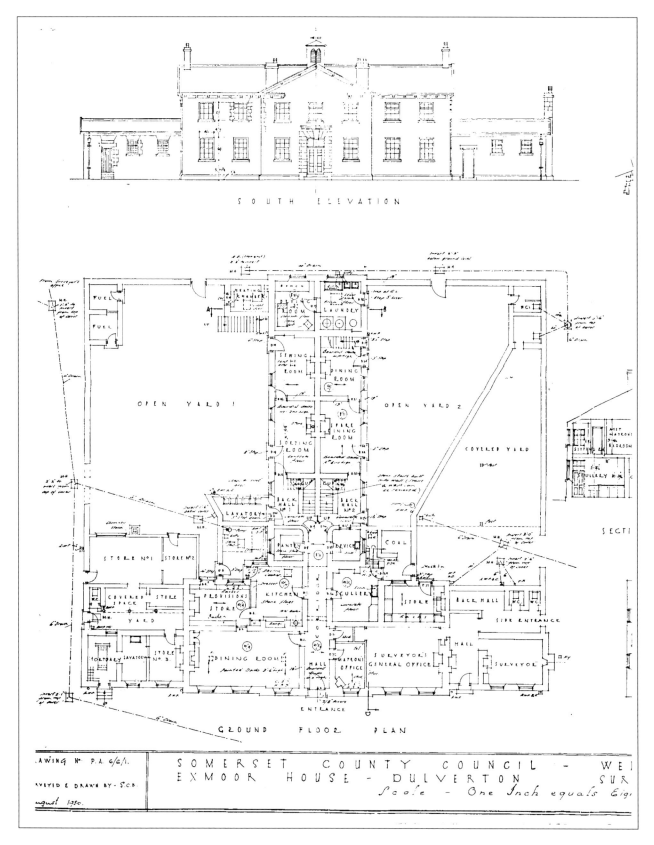

SOUTH ELEVATION

GROUND FLOOR PLAN

on. While Dulverton had a good reputation for being generous – the Guardians were told off once for providing more poor-relief per pauper than any other in Devon and Somerset – they had to toe a rather rigid line.

Discipline resulted in corporal punishment, sometimes solitary confinement and, now and then,

the universal prison regime of bread and water. Porridge, if you were lucky, was something you might have had for breakfast. Charles Dickens famously made Oliver Twist ask for 'more, please sir', a plea that may have applied to many of the paupers who were entitled, under the regulations, to full rations. The problem was that no-one knew just

A Dulverton character, photographed by Hyla Catford, early 1900s.

what a 'full ration' entailed, hence most people were hungry most of the time.

Work was, even then, a four letter word. Men worked on the allotments and the gardens, and the tramps and vagrants were expected to break stones to produce gravel, to pay for their keep. A public leaflet issued on 26 August 1896 stipulated that male casuals 'will be required to break into gravel 4 cwt. of stone per day and pass it through a 7/8in. grating.' Women casuals, on the other hand, had the less onerous job of picking oakum. The Guardians' Clerk, one W.F.B. Dawe, in the leaflet's final paragraph, gave warning that the rules would be rigorously applied. You can almost hear his voice echoing down the years. Mr Dawe ordained (he was only obeying orders): 'No casual pauper will be discharged before the morning of the second day following admission, nor until he or she has performed the prescribed task.'

Changing times and social improvements, like the introduction of an Old Age Pension in 1908, reduced the number of inmates. Official records, for instance, show that in October 1914, only 20 persons were residing in the house. There were, however, 25 vagrants in the building, plus some 'lunatics and idiots'.

Former Assistant Matron Katherine Billing, the daughter of the last Master and Mistress of the workhouse, was responsible for the cooking and the care of the women and children from 1925 until 1929. She provides us with a snapshot of life at Exmoor House in those days, noting:

The day began about 7.00am with preparations for breakfast at 7.30am. In the kitchen, food was served out on a long table, where it was weighed and carried into the dining room. The bell inside the door was rung for meal-times. Breakfast was porridge, bread and dripping and tea. For dinner they might serve vegetable stew and for tea there might be bread and dough cake.

Some of the women did the washing-up and the housework, laying fires in every room, helping with the laundry and ironing with flat irons. The women wore blue and white striped dresses with a white waist apron and a white mob cap.

The tramps, about five or six a day, came for bread and cheese and cocoa at night. There had to stay two

nights and get a bath, which they disliked. They had to report to the Police Station and, if the Police wanted them for any offence, they could arrest them. If not, each tramp received a ticket for a bread and cheese station. This would be Brompton Regis for a tramp going to Williton.

The County Council took over Exmoor House in 1929 and in 1930 all the inmates were transferred to Williton. Tramps were still accommodated, earning their keep by breaking stone, but it was a short reprieve, for, by 1934, the building became a training centre for orphaned girls who were earmarked for domestic service. In 1940 it became a maternity home for London evacuees escaping the Blitz. Many were unmarried mothers, a status which was frowned upon in those unenlightened days.

The old workhouse saw many changes over the following years with the major changes which took place in local government. It was the home of Dulverton Rural District Council until that authority was absorbed into the new West Somerset District Council in 1974. Today it is the headquarters of Exmoor National Park – formed in 1954 – an organisation dedicated to the conservation of this beautiful part of the world, and to supporting the community.

EXMOOR NATIONAL PARK

Soon after the Second World War, the Government decided that it was important to preserve wild and beautiful landscapes to prevent countryside being built over or lost in other ways. It was also thought that everybody, especially those living in cities, should have the opportunity to visit the country and enjoy the fresh air, freedom and scenery. Exmoor was chosen as a National Park because of its size and scenery and also because it was one of the few wild areas in the south of England that people from London, the Midlands and South Wales could visit easily. At the time there were worries that parts of Exmoor might be lost by being planted with conifers, and that unsightly buildings were spoiling the farms and villages. One present-day problem is that too many visitors can lead to traffic congestion and to footpath and bridleway erosion.

The Exmoor National Park Authority's responsibilities are: to conserve and enhance the Parks' natural beauty, wildlife and cultural heritage; to promote opportunities for the public's understanding and enjoyment of the special qualities of the Parks; and to pursue these objectives whilst seeking to foster the social and economic well-being of the local communities.

EIGHT

HUNTING

Hunting in one form or another has taken place around Dulverton and the surrounding area since the Iron Age, and, at the time of writing, is under threat. For the Saxons, this was one of their more favoured hunting lands. Harold made it his own and therefore William claimed it after him. Only the king, his guests and a favoured few could hunt the king's forests. Dulverton and the surrounding area were within one of the royal forests – Exmoor – until 1279, when Dulverton was declared outside the 'pale'. The boundary had moved, though not the forest. The king had bestowed the area upon one of his knights and declared him 'Lord of the Free Manor and Hundred of Dulverton'. A forest – in the old and legal meaning of the word – was simply a district in which the deer and certain other wild animals were reserved for the king and protected by Forest Law.

There are many hunts on and around Exmoor, most being very familiar to the people of Dulverton. A hunt was often invited into the town in past years for different celebrations. The only meet within the town now is on Boxing-Day morning when many people in the town turn out as supporters.

The best known local hunts are the Devon and Somerset Staghounds and what is now the Dulverton Farmers' Hunt, formerly known as the Dulverton Foxhounds (East) Hunt – the name changed in 2001 to reflect the membership. This hunt, which started in 1875, extended from Bampton in the east to Ilfracombe in the west and covered about 12 miles north to south. Later, when Lord Poltimore resigned the Mastership, the hunt was divided into Dulverton East and Dulverton West, with the boundary at Hawkridge. The kennels are at East Anstey.

The Town Hall steps, 1934, with the Devon and Somerset Staghounds.
In the foreground are Albert Cochram and Fred Hawkins as boys.

Stag Hunt resolution, 1840

STAG HUNT.

To the NOBLEMEN and GENTLEMEN of the Counties of DEVON and SOMERSET

At a meeting held at the WHITE HART INN, at DULVERTON, on Tuesday the 19th of May , 1840

The Honble NEWTON FELLOWES in the Chair,

IT WAS RESOLVED ;

1.   That it is most desirable a PACK OF HOUNDS should be kept in or near DULVERTON, for the sole purpose of HUNTING THE WILD DEER.

2.   That with this intention, a Subscription has been entered into by many admirers of that noble Sport, to protect the Deer, and to eatablish a Hunt on a scale in accordance with theexpectations of the Subscribers, and its Friends.

3.   That notwithstanding the call was responded to, yet the Subscriptions and Donations have not been sufficient to effect its purpose, or to place the Hunt in the position which would render it most effective, and at the same time call forth the resources of Sport which lie within its reach; want of funds alone has cramped its management and character.

4.   That with the view of the extension of Country, popularity of the hunt, its welfare and its pleasures, Deer have been conveyed to distant Covers every way suitable to their habits,and where they have bred; and it is the intention of the committee to save instead of destroying the Deer taken by Hounds, in order to afford diversion to other and more distant districts. By these arrangements a great increase of Sport will be afforded, not only to the old Stag Hunters of the Moor, but will also bring this noble Sport within reach of a large body of Sporting men, hitherto strangers to the Hunting of the Stag.

5.   That this meeting puts it to the Noblemen, Gentleman, and others, of the Counties of Devon and Somerset, whether the noble pastime of Hunting the Wild Red Deer in their native Country is to be abandoned because a small increase to the present Funds are wanting to carry it on; SPORTSMEN OF THE WEST SHOULD THIS BE? The Hunt once down never will rise again, and this meeting cannot conceal from themselves and others, their perfect conviction that the safety of the Deer within the Woods and Covers of the Proprietors, and of which they have justly reason to be proud, depend upon and are co-existing with the continuance and prosperity of the NORTH DEVON AND SOMERSET STAGHOUNDS.

6.   That these Resolutions be printed, and a copy be sent to the Noblemen, Gentlemen, and others of the two Counties, with a request that an answer be forwarded to the Secretary and Treasurer, C. P. COLLYNS, Esq. of Dulverton, before the Fourteenth day of August next, to which day this meeting is adjourned.

BY ORDER OF THE MEETING,

N. FELLOWS,
CHAIRMAN

Kings Corner meet, 1914. The two boys in front are Pat and Jack Catford.
Left to right: *Miss L. Fry, Mrs Ethel Catford, Polly Fry, ?.*

Meet in Fore Street, outside the Town Hall, early 1920s.

Above: *Meets above Hele Bridge.*

Right: *Hele Bridge meet, 5 December 1922.*

Below: *Devon and Somerset Staghounds at Haddon, 1920s.*

Above: *Dulverton East Foxhounds, 1940s. The Master is Mr Whitmore of Frogwell Farm, the owner of the kennels and hounds until his death.*

Right: *The head of Big Haddon (the stag) at Hineham Farm, with eight-year-old Jean Campbell.*

Below: *Dulverton East (Farmers) Foxhounds Boxing Day Meet, late 1990s. The huntsman is Anthony Allibone, known as 'Bones'.*

Exford Horse Show, 1967, with Sidney Westcott and Harold Heard.

Somerset County Council butter-making Class held at Beasley Farm, Dulverton, from 24 October until 4 November 1927 – such classes were held at several farms during the 1920s and '30s.

NINE

FARMING

Cattle and sheep breeding and rearing have been the mainstay and backbone of Dulverton and the surrounding area for several hundred years. Farming has created a living not only for the farmers and agricultural workers, but also for all the subsidiary services and businesses linked to it – wheelwrights, wagon makers, thatchers, blacksmiths, harness makers, millers and corn and feed merchants. These days farming relies much more on mechanical appliances and much less on labour.

Some of the farms in the area were well established in Saxon times, including Brofford, Wellway, and Ashway, while others have formed part of large estates – Perry Farm, Gulland, Nightcott, Beasley, Liscombe and Draydon, not forgetting North Combe, with generations of farming families like the Vellacotts, Rawles, Westcotts and Heards.

One of the best known was Sidney Westcott for his breeding and re-establishment of the Exmoor Pony herd on Exmoor – an ancient breed of very hardy pony.

Unfortunately, from time to time Foot and Mouth disease raises its ugly head on Exmoor. This was particularly the case in 2001 and the effects of that outbreak are still, at the time of writing, being strongly felt.

A letter sent to the Heritage Centre recently (2001), from Mrs Joyce Colivet (née Macdonald) tells of how she and her sister were evacuated to Perry Farm from London during the war:

It was all very strange to us of course. We couldn't understand the country accent. There were two farm hands that I remember – Frank and Jim – who gave us rides on old 'Smart'. Mr and Mrs Perry were very kind

Round-up of the Anchor Exmoor Ponies, led by Sid Westcott, 1973.

to us and we had a good time playing in the orchard. I remember too skating on the frozen river in our wellington boots; the new-born lambs and calves; visiting Taunton Cattle Market in the pony and trap; harvest time when the locals came to help kill the rabbits with their guns and large sticks; and helping to pluck the turkeys at Christmas time. I also remember washing with the water from the stone hot water bottles – it was still tepid in the morning... How times have changed!

Changing patterns, or diversification, are always with us in the ever-present industry of farming, thus the countryside as we know it today has evolved.

Hill farming changes least of all mainly because of the higher altitude and weather conditions, often wetter and what seem to be shorter summers and growing periods, and the resultant predominance of livestock. Because of this some of the ancient woodlands have survived around Dulverton, with obvious man management. The beef and sheep breeding has produced some of the most sought-after stock by the lowland farmers.

Since the 1950s tractors and other mechanical aids, both large and small, have been seen more and more on the hills as less and less labour has been available or affordable. Horses have for many years had a favoured place in and around Dulverton, but in more recent years many more are to be seen as some farms are catering for visitors who wish to ride out, and some are providing livery for those who have no stable or grass keep but wish to own a horse for their pleasure and leisure. Exmoor is a marvellous place to explore on horseback, with areas accessible only to those who ride or walk. It does, however, need the farmer to use and care for it.

Haymaking at Nightcott, 1951.

*Fred Rawle and helpers at
East Nightcott, 1951.*

John Hancox, Liscombe Farm, 1947.

Ashway Farm, the birthplace of Sir George Williams, founder of the YMCA.

John Vellacott with children Maurice, Margaret and Patricia.

Above: *Maurice Vellacott (aged 14) with rams at Perry Farm, 1964.*

Right: *Back from hunting, John Vellacott with son Maurice at Perry Farm, 1959.*

Raising funds for the Red Cross, early 1900s.

Red Cross fund-raising, 29 November 1917.

TEN

CLUBS, GROUPS & SOCIETIES

THE EXMOOR SOCIETY

In the 1950s, despite the creation of the National Parks, threats to the wildness and natural beauty of Exmoor were very real. A proposal by the Forestry Commission to plant a conifer forest on open moorland in the heart of the moor aroused strong opposition from lovers of Exmoor. Further concern surrounded the rate at which moorland was being ploughed and fenced by landowners, aided by grants from the then Ministry of Agriculture. In response to these threats, it was decided to found a voluntary society to campaign for conservation and to make the issues more widely known.

The Exmoor Society was formed in 1959, in alliance with the Council for the Preservation of Rural England. The early years were dominated by battles between the Society on one side and landowners and farmers – and often the National Park Committee of the day – on the other. The diminishing acreage of open moorland became a matter of public concern. This led to the Portchester Inquiry which reported in 1977, and whose recommendations were largely implemented in the Wildlife and Countryside Act 1981. Thus began the move towards the protection of open countryside, assisted where necessary by subsidies and other environmental help. The Society supports most of the policies and actions of the National Park Authority, although there are still occasional differences.

Today there are over 2,600 members, many of them from well outside Exmoor. It employs two part-time officers (the Secretary and the Membership Secretary) and has a turnover of over £30,000 a year. With groups in Dulverton, South Molton, Barnstaple, Combe Martin, Bristol and London, the Society's major tasks are: to scrutinise local plans and planning applications; to act as a watchdog by promoting the conservation of land, woodland, river systems and the coast; to ensure access to the open country and the use of well-maintained rights of way; to encourage the understanding and responsible enjoyment of Exmoor by its visitors; and to organise regular events for its members, lectures, seminars, moorland walks, and socials, as well as the Annual General Meeting.

FRIENDLY SOCIETIES

The Dulverton area had three Friendly Societies from the early 1800s. This was most unusual for a town of its size, with a population of between 1,400 and 1,500. The Dulverton Friendly Society was formed in the year 1816 with a membership of about 80, and remained in existence for over 150 years. The Rational Association Friendly Society, originating in 1837 in Manchester, had members in Dulverton until it disbanded in 1925.

Such Societies became numerous in the nineteenth century in Britain, members paying regular contributions and, in return, receiving financial aid in sickness or old age and on death. Many closed after 1948 when National Insurance contributions were introduced, but the Dulverton Friendly Society, which in 1897 had a membership of 300, continued until 1967.

In 1856 it acquired all the land and a cottage behind the Bridge Inn. This land became gardens or allotments and extended from the Bridge Inn right to Addlemead. The area is now occupied by the Fire Station, the Police Station and former police houses, car park, Caravan Club and Hanover Court. Members could rent the gardens for a nominal sum and the Club depended on the income from this property and from the one shilling a month contributions of its members. At the end of the year, if there was a surplus, it would be divided each Whit Monday among the members. The strongbox where funds were kept had five locks, with one key for the Secretary and one each for the four stewards. According to the rules, the box could not be opened until all the stewards were present or had sent a deputy, as all the keys were different. One steward living at Hineham Cottages at the top of Northmoor Hill forgot his key and had to walk the five miles return journey before the meeting could proceed.

In 1928 the cottage needed repair, which left the Club in debt to the extent of £150. This was cleared by selling the cottage for £300 and war loans were purchased with the remaining £150.

Until 1930, there was a Club Walk each Whit Monday, which all the members had to attend; they

Red Cross

Left: *Outside Parish Rooms, 1954.*
Left to right, back: *Lucy Westcott, ? Hart, Kathleen Nelder, Mrs Bonham Carter, Mrs Mary Smail (Commandant), Hilda Andrews, Mrs Jean Campbell, Patsy du Boe, Betty Baker, Eileen Thomas, Ivy Bidgood, Mary Rendell;* middle: *?, June Blacklock, Vivienne Lang, Josie How, Betty Wood, evacuee;* seated: *Jean Chanter, Margaret Stevens, Carol Govier, ?, Tessa Newton, Beryl Mountstevens, ?, Lorna Rowcliffe.*

Above left: *First Aid Post at Dunster Castle.* Standing: *Jean Campbell, Mary Rendell;* seated: *Ena Luxton, Lucy Westcott, Mary Smail (Commandant), Kathleen Nelder.*

Above: *Winning the County Cup, 1966/67.* Left to right: *Jean Campbell, Stephanie Herbert, ?, Caroline Stanbury, Diana Campbell, Mary Rendell;* Cadets with cups: *? Collard, Felicity Rendell.*

Below: *Red Cross Golden Jubilee, Wells Cathedral, 1960, the Duchess of Kent inspecting. Mary Rendell is second from right.*

Above: *Red Cross County Competition, c.1970.* Left to right, standing: *Pam Sparkes and Hilda Andrews;* seated: *Mary Rendell, Jean Campbell, Mary Smail.*

had to wear rosettes in their hats, or be fined. They met in the square where their names were called by a steward. They then lined up outside the Town Hall behind the senior member with the banner, the inscription on which read, 'Bear ye one another's burdens'. Then with the Town Band leading, the procession circled the town, and proceeded to the church for their annual service – and the risk of being reminded by the vicar that he had not seen them in church since the previous Whit Monday! The service was followed by a dinner and liquid consumption at one of the local hotels.

Membership began to dwindle once the National Insurance scheme was established and, in 1967, numbers had dropped to 14. As the contributions and garden rents were falling, the trustees and stewards decided it would be best to disband, according to the book of rules of the club.

The gardens were sold to the Town Council and the banner placed into the care of Taunton Museum in 1968.

Ancient Order of Foresters Friendly Society

This Friendly Society was country-wide and founded in 1834, possibly arriving in Dulverton a year or so later. The branch was named Court Northmoor and was connected with and formed part of the Exeter District Branch of the Order, their aims and benefits being similar to those of the Dulverton Friendly Society. Their meetings were held in the Lamb Hotel and continued for 150 years.

SCOUTS & GUIDES

The earliest of these youth groups has to be the Scouts, which was created by Baden Powell in 1908, the movement spreading very rapidly throughout the country. Dulverton's first troop was formed with great enthusiasm in 1908 and continues to this day. The Girl Guide movement was not established until 1910, but was no doubt taken up equally enthusiastically by Dulverton girls. Now we have the Rainbows, as well as the Brownies and Guides.

THE RED CROSS ASSOCIATION

Fund-raising for the Red Cross Association took place in Dulverton from the time of its inception in Britain in 1910. Dulverton ladies were accustomed to raising funds through fêtes or auctions for good causes and, in July 1901, a successful jumble sale was held at the Town Hall in aid of the Nursing Fund. Several ladies took part and raised £16.8s.11d. In 1946 Mrs P.C. Collins of Dulverton was one of a number of ladies presented with Distinguished War Service Certificates on behalf of the Red Cross.

From 1946 onwards, the Red Cross Association in Dulverton grew in strength – both cadets and seniors

– with each group winning competitions at local and county level. During the Red Cross Golden Jubilee in 1960, members of the Dulverton group were in the line-up to meet the Duchess of Kent at Wells.

BRITISH LEGION

The first meeting of past comrades of the Great War was held in Dulverton on 14 August 1918. However, the inaugural meeting was not held until 16 September 1921 in the Parish Rooms, when the constitution of the British Legion was adopted and a local committee voted in with Mr C.F. Foster as Chairman and Mr A. Ford as Secretary. Capt. Lionel Popkiss was Chairman of the branch from September 1927 until January 1936, by which time there were 178 members. Mr A.J. Balsom was Secretary.

Col E. Harrison of Combe and Col E. Clayton served as Presidents between 1926–63, taking turns to fill this office until Col Clayton's death in 1957. Col Harrison died in 1963, having given the Legion House (Hall) and Page House to the group in 1954.

The Queen granted the prefix Royal to the Legion to mark the 50th Anniversary in July 1971. In November 1983, Lt Cdr Caetlidge, Captain of HMS *Dulverton*, and members of his crew came to the Armistice Service held at All Saints in commemoration of the sinking of HMS *Dulverton* on 13 November 1943. Mr John Lowes has been standard bearer since 1982.

At the November 1993 Remembrance Service, the Captain of HMS *Dulverton* came not with his crew, but with eight survivors of the original HMS *Dulverton* sunk in 1943.

British Legion march for the commemoration service, 15 June 1997, at which there were 150 members with their banners.

Ꮙᎇ *Scouts* Ꮙᎇ

Above: *Scouts Parade at Dunster Castle, c.1936/8. Standing at back:* Mr Munday, Scoutmaster, Charlie Warren; *from the left:* Dick Steer, Stan Mathews, Jim Blackmore, Dick Puttock, Jimmy Herniman, Charlie Mathews, Archie Hoskins, Gordon Crocker, John Ford, Charlie Burton, Douglas Gunter, Jim Burton, Douglas Litton, Ron Mathews, Sonny Gammon, Bill Durman.

Above: *Dulverton Boy Scouts at Camp at Dawlish 1947/8. Left to right, back:* Arthur Andrews (Scout-master), Bob Coggins, Ashley Starks, John Biggs, Bruce Kemp, Michael Starks, Alan Steer, Alan Baker, Herbert Waterman, Archie Chanter, Sidney Waterman, Alan Mitchell; *front:* Ken Norman, John Huxtable, Patrick Bird, Pete Andrews, Owen Rowcliffe, Pat Chanter, Brian Smith.

Above: *Dulverton First Scout Troop presented with Colours on The Pound, 1907/8, with proud parents.*

Guides

Above: *Empire Youth Sunday 9 May 1948. 'Brown Owl' at the front is Joan Page.*

Right: *Rotary presenting a cheque for £100 to 1st Dulverton Girl Guides, 1988.*

Below: *Congregational Church Brownies/Guides Parade, early 1980s (?).*

✺ Friendly & Exmoor Societies ✺

Above: *Dulverton Friendly Society, after winding up in 1968, handing their banner into the care of Taunton Museum via the Mayor of Taunton. The 2nd from left: representative from Taunton Museum; 3rd: Nip Chanter; 5th: Mayor, Mr Snow and W. Parker.*

Left: *Launching of* Essence of Exmoor *by Victor Bonham Carter.*

Below: *David and Richard from North Devon College, Barnstaple, in front of their display – both spoke at the Exmoor Society AGM, 2001.*

Below left: *Exmoor Society AGM 1999 – President Victor Bonham Carter and Chairman Michael Hawkins, with Keith Bungay – retiring from Exmoor National Park.*

Some 16 members of the Legion took part in the *Land Girls* film – some as Home Guard members, others as Air Raid Wardens. The Committee at the time of writing is as follows:

President:	Revd A.R.N. Appleby
Chairman:	Mr D. Williams
Hon. Secretary:	Mr A. Walker
Hon. Treasurer:	Mr G. Poat
Welfare Secretary:	Mrs M. Atkins
Standard Bearer:	Mr J. Lowes
Poppy Appeal Organiser:	Mr M. Atkins

The Dulverton Branch covers the area of Dulverton, Brompton Regis, Bury, part of Exebridge, Hawkridge, Withypool, Exford and Simonsbath.

DULVERTON & SOUTHERN EXMOOR TWINNING ASSOCIATION

This Association evolved from the Dulverton Project – an informal link-up of contacts in National Parks around the world – which identified the need for an international forum for sharing expertise in rural development. The Dulverton Network was set up in 1995, incorporating the rural communities of Artea in Spain, Zwierzyniec in Poland and St Laurent de Neste in France, as founder members. In 1998, the Twinning Association of the four communities was formally established. Their specific aim was to ensure that the voices of small, rural communities could be heard in Brussels more effectively in combination. In 1999, Dulverton received a Golden Star award from the European Union for innovation and initiative in furthering international cooperation – an outstanding achievement, as it was one of only 14 awards to be made from a total of 17,000 twinning associations throughout Europe.

Exmoor National Park and Dulverton Middle and Community School are firmly committed partners, as much of the work of the Association is concerned with exchange visits for young people and conservation volunteers. Regular seminars are hosted in turn by the four communities. They discuss and share experience of mutual interests in sustainable tourism, the marketing of local produce, preserving cultural identity and – a very topical theme – the concept of active volunteering as a feature of rural development to complement the 'us and them' philosophy of peasant independence.

OTHER GROUPS

The Bicycle Club started in 1893 and, at the end of their first season, presented prizes for attendance to G. Hawkins, G. Stacey and F. Parminter. The Working Men's Club, the Rifle Range Club, and the Football and Cricket Clubs all started around the same time. Later came Angling and Deep-Sea Angling, the Camera Club and Dulverton Art Group. Later still came the Rotary. Fairly early on, between 1919 and 1939, other groups such as the Women's Institute, and the Mothers' Union were formed in Dulverton. Most of these are still ongoing.

Right: *Artea, September 1998; the unveiling of the monolith in the twinning garden to commemorate twinning of the four towns.*

Left: *Bilbao 1999 Twinning Ceremony with Chairman Pat Skipper. Left to right: Jaries Beitia of Artea, Spain, Marek Marcola of Zwierzyniec, Poland, Pat Skipper (Chairman, Dulverton Council), Jacques Birabert of St Laurent de Neste, France.*

A Presentation at Dulverton Camera Club, 1968.

The Billiard Room, Working Men's Club, and a match between Fisher and Bickell, early 1900s. Bickell, known as 'General Bickell', is at the table.

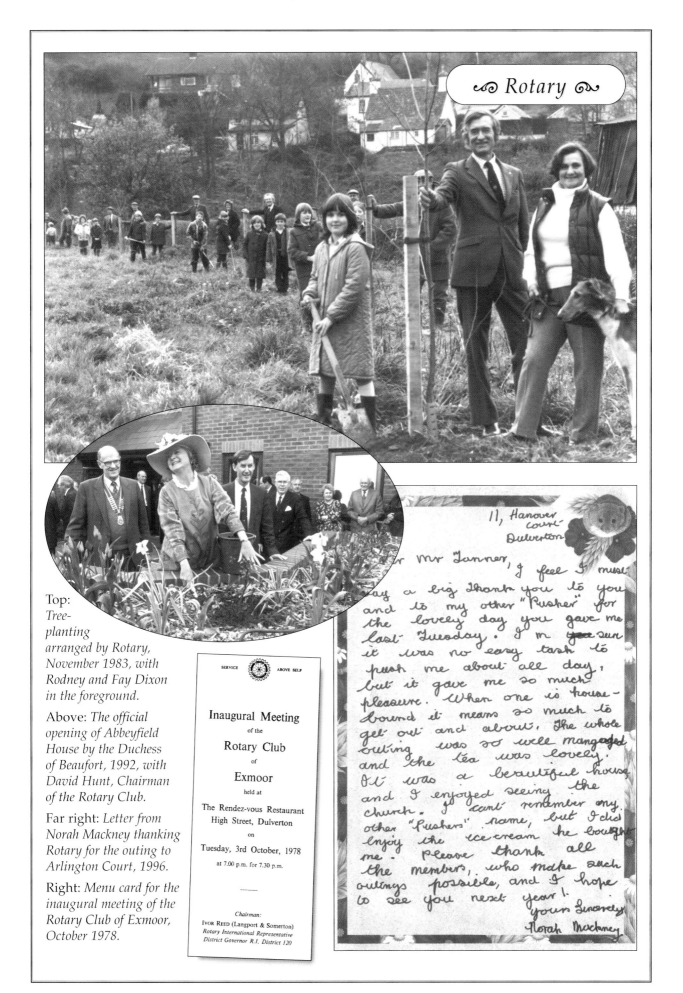

Rotary

Top:
*Tree-
planting
arranged by Rotary,
November 1983, with
Rodney and Fay Dixon
in the foreground.*

Above: *The official
opening of Abbeyfield
House by the Duchess
of Beaufort, 1992, with
David Hunt, Chairman
of the Rotary Club.*

Far right: *Letter from
Norah Mackney thanking
Rotary for the outing to
Arlington Court, 1996.*

Right: *Menu card for the
inaugural meeting of the
Rotary Club of Exmoor,
October 1978.*

SERVICE ABOVE SELF

Inaugural Meeting
of the

Rotary Club
of

Exmoor
held at

The Rendez-vous Restaurant
High Street, Dulverton
on

Tuesday, 3rd October, 1978

at 7.00 p.m. for 7.30 p.m.

Chairman:
IVOR REED (Langport & Somerton)
*Rotary International Representative
District Governor R.I. District 120*

11, Hanover
court
Dulverton

Dear Mr Tanner, I feel I must
say a big Thank you to you
and to my other "Pusher" for
the lovely day you gave me
last Tuesday. I'm sure
it was no easy task to
push me about all day,
but it gave me so much
pleasure. When one is house-
bound it means so much to
get out and about. The whole
outing was so well managed
and the tea was lovely.
It was a beautiful house
and I enjoyed seeing the
church. I can't remember any
other "Pushers" name, but I did
enjoy the ice-cream he bought
me. Please thank all
the members, who make such
outings possible, and I hope
to see you next year!
yours sincerely
Norah Mackney

~ *Football* ~

Above: *Dulverton Football Team, 1931–33.* The players were: *Fred Williams, Frank Lang, Jack Hobbs, Jack German, Sid Huxtable, Charlie Cridge, Jack Andrews (goal), Fred Patterson, Albert Denning, Fred Harris, Buck Pollard (with cup), Drummer Ford, Alex Ford.*

Right: *Dulverton Football Team, 1922–23. Third from left, centre, is Jack Warren.*

Below: *Dulverton Football Team, 1912–13.* Left to right, back: *H. Broom, A. Horn, H. Page, W. Wethers, A. Balsom, G. Lugg, W. Radcliffe, H. Ebsworth;* middle: *G. Hobbs, E. Ford, L. Kingdon (Capt.), F. Martin (Sub Capt.), F. Hicks;* front: *E. Marsh, W. Grant, H. Bale.*

Above: *Dulverton Football Club, 1906–07.*

Right: *Dulverton Football Club, 1925.*

Below: *Dulverton Football Club, late 1940s.*

Bottom right: *Dulverton Football Club with five cups, c.1950.*

Bottom left: *John Ridler, Somerset County Youth Team, 1948. He played for Arsenal, playing in goal for England against Holland in 1949.*

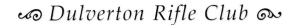

❧ Dulverton Rifle Club ❧

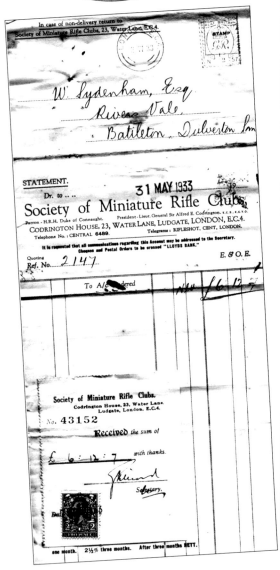

Left: *Presentation of award to Sian Massie, aged 17, by the Chief Constable, Thames Valley Police, at Bisley in 1984. Sian was the top Junior Shooter (aggregate over four days).*

Below: *Great Britain Shooting Squad, 1985, European Shooting Championship, Ozijek, Yugoslavia – one of the competitors came from Dulverton.*

Below right: *Rent receipt of the Rifle Range paid to Pixton Estate, 1936.*

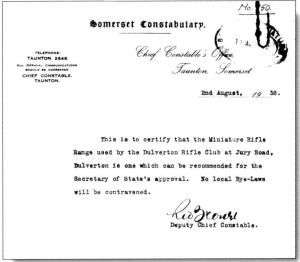

Above: *Receipt from the Society of Miniature Rifle Clubs for their membership of the Dulverton Club, 1933.*

Right: *Permission dated August 1938 by Somerset Constabulary for the range used by the Dulverton Rifle Club.*

Cricket

Cricket players, early 1940s.
Left to right: Jim Blackmore, Stan Mathews, Freddie Hawkins, Pat Patterson, Jimmy Herniman.

Dulverton Cricket team, 1983. Left to right,
back: Mike Lloyd, Will Hobbs, Phil Cottrill,
Nick Blundell, David Bodger, Steve Ridler;
front: Steve Hayes, ?, Bob Scoins (with cap),
Steve Howe, John Woodman.

Dulverton Cricket team, 1993.
Left to right, back: Graham Kingdon, ?, Kevin Kingdon,
Matthew (?) Pershouse, ?;
middle: Stewart Gayle, Pete Cockram, Richard Drewer;
seated: ? Drewer, Mike Gammon, Carl Drewer.

Carnarvon Arms Hotel with Carnarvon Arms Garage in the middle distance to the left after 1912.
Note that there is as yet no road link leading from the garage to the right to Perry Bridge.

Carnarvon Arms Hotel, c.1904. The thatched summerhouse is long gone.
In the background visitors to the hotel can be seen. In the foreground are Smith the gardener (note the push
mower which was a little inadequate for this enormous lawn), George Nelder in the centre with the wheelbarrow
and a group, to the right, consisting of, **from left to right:** *Molly Nelder, Winifred Nelder, Ida Nelder,*
Miss Webber (the Nelder children's governess).

ELEVEN
⌒⊙⌒

CARNARVON ARMS HOTEL, STATION, GARAGE & THE NELDER FAMILY

By 1844, the railway had reached Taunton. Brunel had planned that the North Devon Railway should run from the Bristol and Exeter line at Hillfarrance through to Barnstaple. However, like so many railway lines projected during railway mania, it proved to be abortive. In 1863, Brunel's scheme was modified by another railway engineer, Eugenius Birch. This was to be known as the Devon and Somerset Railway, to run from Norton Fitzwarren to Barnstaple, along the previously planned route. A year later – after the appropriate Act was passed and the necessary borrowing powers were obtained – the first sod was cut by Lady Poltimore on the site of South Molton Station. The gauge, or the width, of the track was to be 7ft, i.e. broad gauge.

By August 1866, the Norton Fitzwarren section had been staked out and work was continuing on the South Molton section. After five years of trouble with strikes, bad weather and lack of capital, the railway was opened from Norton Fitzwarren to Wiveliscombe via Milverton on 8 June 1871. The price of rails had risen from £8 to £14 per ton during June 1872 and wet weather again held up progress.

In July 1873, the Earl of Carnarvon – the then owner of Pixton Park – built a free market close to Dulverton Station, no tolls being charged. However, this did not please those in Dulverton who would lose their town market trade. He also built the Carnarvon Arms Hotel to further the prosperity of the new market and finished building it in 1874.

Four in Hand Coach known as the Tally Ho used between Dulverton Station and Dulverton Town, c.1880

James and Ann Nelder were the first tenants and licensees and came to it after leaving the Black Horse public house in Tiverton. In 1877, on James' death, he was succeeded by his son Charles William, who continued to run the hotel with his mother. When she died in 1889, Charles married Edith, a schoolmistress from Bristol, who then had to learn the business, which they ran together. Between 1890 and 1900, they had six children – four girls and two boys. The elder son, Reginald, was later to take over the running of the hotel, while the younger son, George, assisted with the home farm. Charles William was a restless and inventive man, who built up the hotel business, tried a number of sidelines and, in a deal with the Carnarvon Estate, expanded the hotel and stables. As stag hunting on Exmoor became more popular, it was possible to 'box' horses down from other parts of the country by rail, as the railway was now well established.

The regular train service started on 1 November 1873. To celebrate the opening, triumphal arches were erected at Dulverton, bells were rung and there was a bonfire, with fireworks in the evening. There was a further special celebration in August 1874, when free tickets were issued to gentlemen and farmers to travel to Dulverton, and 200 guests dined in the Dulverton Station goods shed.

Of course you would expect the railway station to be at the location of the town's name, but Dulverton does not come into this category. You – as a visitor to

Above and right: *Two photographs of Dulverton Station in 1928.*

Below: *Old and new cranes at the station in the same year.*

Railway Days

Top: *Dulverton Station, Carnarvon Arms Hotel and Pixton, before 1910.*

Above: *Helicopter in the snow taking animal feed to the fields, landing beside the station, 1963.*

Above right: *Dulverton Station without travellers.*

Right: *'The last train from Dulverton', a postcard of 1908.*

Left: *The earliest Carnarvon Arms Garage.*

Below: *GWR lorry, driven by Jack Vellacott, Dulverton Station, 1928.*

Bottom right and below left: *Carnarvon Arms garage tariff, July 1910.*

WIRE SPENCER, DULVERTON. Phone Nº 2.

The CARNARVON ARMS GARAGE, DULVERTON, SOMERSET.

MOTOR HIRE TARIFF.

Above: *Carnarvon Arms Garage Annual Outing to the Pantomime in the New Hall, Tiverton, c.1964.*
Picture includes: *Ivy Bidgood, Charley Bidgood, Mickey Hammond, Chris Nelder, Ray Quartley, Nancy Quartley, Eve Wotton, Edward Wotton, John Bidgood, Betty Thomas, Jean Woodcock, Mr Hammond, Vic Woodcock, ? Thomas; seated: Bettye Nelder, Kathleen Nelder, George Nelder, Bailey ?, Mrs Hammond; front: Garry Nelder, William Hutter, Julie Hutter, Jennifer Nelder, Suzanne Nelder, Brian Woodcock, Mickey Hutter, Mike Quartley.*

The Carnarvon Arms Garage.

MOTOR HIRE TARIFF: JULY, 1910.

LARGE CAR (35-45 h.p. Gladiator).

To Seat up to Six Passengers, besides Driver.

	£	s.	d.
Per Day of 12 Hours (up to 100 Miles, 1/- per Mile over) ...	5	5	0
Per Half-day of 6 Hours (up to 50 Miles, 1/- per Mile over)	2	15	0
Per Mile		1	0
Returning Empty (10 Miles allowed at 6d.) per Mile over...		1	0
Waiting, per Hour		2	0

SMALL CAR (12-14 h.p. Gladiator).

To Seat up to Three Passengers, besides Driver.

	£	s.	d.
Per Day of 12 Hours (up to 100 Miles, 10d. per Mile over)	4	4	0
Per Half-day of 6 Hours (up to 50 Miles, 10d. per Mile over)	2	7	6
Per Mile			10
Returning Empty (10 Miles allowed at 5d.) per Mile over ...			10
Waiting, per Hour		2	0

Charges for Longer Periods by Arrangement.

Hirer pays for Petrol, Keep of Driver, and Housing of Car when away from Dulverton for more than One Day.

the station – might ask a local character, 'Why is Dulverton's station two miles out of town on the Brushford road?' The answer probably would have come out something like this: 'Wull, zur, I doan't rightly knaw, but I 'xpects they put thic station there zo as to be near the trains.' In actual fact, the geography of the region is such that for a train to run into Dulverton and on to East Anstey, the next stop down the line, would have been impossible without blowing tunnels through the intervening hills.

During 1881, the Directors had to find £12,941.18s.9d. to change the track from broad gauge to standard gauge. This was necessary as the national railway network was standardising for the interconnection of all the privately-owned railway companies. The work on this line was carried out during one weekend in May.

In 1884, Dulverton Station became a junction when it was joined by the Exe Valley Railway. The station itself was subject to many changes during the course of its history. The track layout was changed according to the demands of its traffic. The next notable date was July 1901 when Great Western Railway purchased the line from the Devon and Somerset Railway for the princely sum of £850,000.

It is interesting to compare the blizzards of 1891 and 1963 to see how the companies handled the situation. Take 1891, and we are told that a snow plough was brought to Barnstaple, but no locomotive to which it could be fitted was available, so the line was closed until the thaw came. Almost 70 years later in 1963, the route was kept open with a snow plough, housed at Taunton, and a helicopter was used to distribute supplies to outlying areas from Dulverton Station for about ten weeks.

During the Second World War, the line was used to transport tanks and other military supplies to Barnstaple and Bideford, both for the Normandy build-up and for invasion rehearsals. Thousands of American troops were stationed on Exmoor and in the surrounding district. An American Lieutenant and six soldiers were continually at work in the goods yard at Dulverton unloading supplies. Shortly before D-Day, General Dwight D. Eisenhower, Commander in Chief of the United States Forces, came down to inspect these troops, his train being stabled at Dulverton 'Up' platform for two or three days. This probably did not please the Great Western Railway as it probably disrupted regular traffic!

With the increase in road transport the line became progressively uneconomic and lost about £80,000 annually. The Beeching Report of 1963 recommended closure of the branch and this was actually scheduled for August 1965. However, it remained open because the Ministry of Transport imposed a condition that an alternative bus service must first be provided. By the time this was implemented it was mid 1966 and the last train ran on 1 October of that year.

An interesting piece was published in the then *Devon & Somerset News* of 7 July 1963:

What started as a light-hearted frolic to give children pleasure and raise some money for Dulverton Primary School Parents' and Teachers' Association was seen on Saturday week to have a useful bearing on Dr. Beeching's assault on the Exe Valley branch railway line. It was a mock-up railway engine, built from odds and ends and mounted on the ancient chassis of a 12 h.p. Rover car by Mr. Christopher Nelder, son of Mr. G.G. Nelder, proprietor of the Carnarvon Arms Garage, Brushford and his friend, Mr. Bob Walker. Both have children at the school and the railway engine was a rush job to feature at the school's annual fête on Saturday week. It was an immediate success and 150 children were given rides around the sports field at 6d. per head.

That night, the big protest meeting against the Beeching proposal was held at Dulverton Town Hall. Chris Nelder and Bob Walker had the happy idea of parking 'The Dulverton Express' outside it. The bits and pieces of which the engine is made include an old cistern found on a scrap heap, an oil drum for a funnel, a telephone insulator for a whistle, an upturned lamp reflector for a pressure escape, almost prehistoric oil lamps, and a shiny brass bell borrowed from The Rock Inn, Dulverton. The colour scheme of black and green and the whole outline of the outfit were based on an illustration in an old railway book.

The piece of ground on which the Carnarvon Arms Garage started life was part of Lord Carnarvon's Estate. The ground was bought in 1908 by the Spencer brothers and a Dutch barn was erected from which to run a motor-repair and sales business, which was in its infancy at the time. The trade grew, and many sides of the business were expanded, including car hire, chauffeuring, carrying goods, etc. Later on in the 1920s, Edward 'Nippy' Anderson took over the garage. He subsequently went into partnership with George Nelder, who was running the Carnarvon Arms Hotel home farm.

In the following years, they formed a limited company, the Carnarvon Arms Garage Ltd, and the company continued to trade on that site until the premises were rebuilt on the southern side of the Brushford Road by the present owners, Mrs Kathleen Nelder – George Nelder's second wife – and his son, Chris Nelder. The premises are, at the time of writing, leased to an agricultural supplier.

The following are a few of the items carried by the *West Somerset Free Press* about the railway and the Carnarvon Arms at the end of the nineteenth century:

8 June 1895
Poles and cables arrived at Dulverton station, along with a party of Royal Engineers, for the start of a scheme to erect a telephone line from the town to Exford.

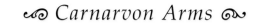

Carnarvon Arms

Above: *The Carnarvon Arms Hotel from the front, photographed during a hunting meet, c.1918.*

Left: *James Nelder (died 1877).*

Below left: *An advertisement from 1912.*

Below: *Charles W. Nelder.*

⊲⊲ **DULVERTON.** ⊳⊳

Moor Driving affords most pleasant Summer Day Excursions.

Good Carriages with Steady Horses and Drivers, SUPPLIED AT MODERATE PRICES BY

NELDER & SON,

CARNARVON ARMS HOTEL.

Among the Chief Points of Interest on the Moor are TARR STEPS, The DEVIL'S PUNCH BOWL, DUNKERRY BEACON, etc. The route to Lynton comprises some of the Finest Scenery in the World. The HOTEL adjoins the Railway Station.

NELDER & SON,

Coal, Coke & Salt Merchants,

DEALERS IN BRICKS OF ALL DESCRIPTIONS, TILES, DRAIN PIPE, SLATE, &C.,

Special Terms quoted for large quantities, Discount for Cash Payments.

Stores adjoining the Carnarvon Arms Hotel.

*Source: Cow Keepers Book
Bound: Dec 1912
For Cow Keeping Guide*

11 January 1896
A Spaniard was arrested on fraud charges by French police after attempting to swindle Mr C.W. Nelder, of the Carnarvon Arms, Dulverton, with a very old trick. He wrote to Mr Nelder from Toulouse charging 51 francs to dispatch non-existent goods.

22 February 1896
A West Somerset widow was granted £300 compensation by the GWR for the loss of her husband when he fell out of a train.

20th November 1897
Dulverton stationmaster Mr Burrows presented passenger guard Mr William Snell with £14.6s.6d. subscribed by the public to mark his retirement after 39 years service.

In the 1920s, Mrs Hoskins of Carnbrae had a young trainee signalman lodging with her. One day, late for duty at 6.30am, and with clothes in disarray, he hurriedly cycled the one and a half miles to the station, only to find the train already there and the passengers leaning out of the windows cheering him on. His duties at that time meant handing on a certain 'key' to the train driver to proceed to the next stop, and releasing the station signal to go. He was never late again.

The *Western Times* of January 1936 recorded a very sad event which had occurred the previous year on 8 January. Under the heading, 'Deaf Mute's Bravery Commemorated – Dulverton Rail Tragedy Recalled', it reads:

The heroic act of a deaf mute, who, unable to raise the alarm or shout a warning when he saw a train at Dulverton railway station bearing down on a mother and child, threw himself in front of the train in a vain endeavour to save their lives, has been commemorated by the erection in the Parish Church of East Anstey, of which place he was a native, of a mural tablet recording the bravery and self-sacrifice of Albert William Tarr, of Buckets Hole, East Anstey. Inset in the tablet are the obverse and reverse sides of the Carnegie Hero bronze medal which was posthumously awarded.

On a happier note, Fred Wilson, who came to Dulverton in 1947, remembers the valuable service provided by the railway:

At that time I used to use the train service at Dulverton a lot to go down to see my father and my mother in Exmouth at weekends – there was a half-hourly service. You could also get to London quite easily – Dulverton was a junction – by going to Tiverton, Taunton or Barnstaple. So although not so many people had cars, more people were more mobile than they are now because of the railway station. Buses used to meet every train and there were three or four taxis. In the early

days it was horse and carriage. A lot of visitors used to come by train and stay at the hotels, like the Carnarvon, for the hunting and fishing seasons, when they were pretty well booked up. Bulk stuff like coal used to come in by train. At one stage, rabbits were taken out by train. Later it was decided to take them by lorry twice a week, picking up the rabbits from the outlying farms. Rabbits were useful for food as meat was in short supply during rationing. People would go to Minehead or perhaps somewhere on the north coast for the day.

The railway station is now closed and is, at the time of writing, being redeveloped. In order to capture the feel of a working station during the busy period of 1935, a scale model, depicting the buildings and the Carnarvon Arms Hotel, is being built at the Heritage Centre in Dulverton. The model will be built on the scale of 4mm to the foot, with trains operated by computer. When it is finished it will be accessible to all.

As a postscript, a survey document dated November 1877 came to light recently showing that a railway was planned between Dulverton and Withypool. This was to be named Barle Valley Railway. The papers referred to:

... an Act to be passed in the Houses of Parliament in 1878, to make and maintain a railway, from a field 40 yards to the north of Marsh Bridge called the Moor, to a field in Withypool called Lower Cleeve.

On examination of the accompanying schedule, it was obvious that the route was to follow the River Barle. Clearly they required the gauge to be other than the standard of the day, as it was noted that they required exemption from 'an Act for Regulating the Gauge of Railways'. The application was signed by Samuel Hayman Warren, Solicitor, Dulverton.

One wonders how that railway was to pay its way from Dulverton to a small village in the moor. Did the impetus come from iron mining, agriculture, or was it just a local whim?

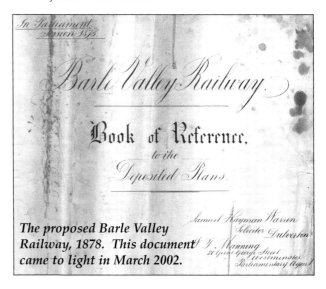

The proposed Barle Valley Railway, 1878. This document came to light in March 2002.

Meet in Fore Street, late 1920s. Note the gloves worn by the policeman in the foreground.

Main: *Dulverton High Street before 1900, showing the Police Station, now Dulverton Pharmacy.*
Inset: *Dr Sydenham.*

TWELVE

❧❦❧

ESSENTIAL SERVICES

PHARMACIES, DOCTORS & VETS

In 1617, the Society of Apothecaries was founded in London – mainly dispensing, but also prescribing their own medicines. During the eighteenth century, chemists and druggists became established within the medical profession. The basis was a shop which sold many things, but chiefly produced pills, potions and lotions. During this period, chemists learned their trade through an apprenticeship in an existing business. In 1841, the Royal Pharmacological Society was founded, keeping a list of members who had passed their exams. In 1868 the Pharmacy Act was passed which required all chemists and druggists to register, in order to practise.

From early times there were many herbalists and druggists in Dulverton, some trading from shops, others from their homes, perhaps with a little witchcraft thrown in! The recognised ones were:

John Ocock (1856–65) *not registered, died aged 33*

Charles Ocock (1865–84) *brother to John, served as an apprentice to him, registered at 18 years old.*

Mary Ocock (1869–90) *John's wife, was registered for 21 years (Mary and Charles had separate establishments)*

George Albert Yates (1889–90) *served as lay preacher in the Methodist Church for many years. Named on the foundation stone of the Chapel in Lady Street*

J. McFadzean (1934–42) *also produced stationery*

R. Towle (1942–48)

P. Profitt (1948–74)

C. Gardiner (1974–99)

The last named were chemists as we know them today. Earlier, they sold many things from knitting patterns to newspapers, magazines and groceries. The Chemists Log Book is on exhibition at the Heritage Centre.

Doctors often used to dispense their own medicines – and still do. Country doctors in days gone by would, if necessary, visit their patients on horseback or by pony and trap. In Dulverton, it was usually on horseback as roads were either appalling or non-existent. If patients lived in town and were able they visited the surgery, which cost slightly less.

Veterinary Surgeons in Dulverton now have a well-established practice with a surgery where Dulverton's ancient pound and pit used to be. The one prior to that was around 1945 in North Moor Road. The premises necessitated a steep climb to the house.

Clockwise from top: *Dr Woodman's Retirement Party. Left to right: Drs F. Ashton, L. Burton, J.D. Peck, J.S. Woodman, R.G. Thomson; Chemist Mr John McFadzean and his wife Christina, 1942; Dr Wilson (centre).*

THE POLICE

There was no regular police force established in Britain until the first one set up by Sir Robert Peel in London in 1829. From medieval times a petty or parish constable was appointed to preserve the peace in his area and to execute the orders of Justices of the Peace. In towns, the 'watch' patrolled and guarded the streets. In Dulverton, granted its first charter in 1278, constables were appointed by the Town Trustees. Their job was to collect tolls from store-holders in the market, the toll-gates of the town, to supervise the weights and measures used by traders and to give help where needed to the tithing men who collected taxes.

By 1740, the Town Trustees appointed a number of Dulverton inhabitants to 'Watch in the Night within the Town and Borough of Dulverton for Aggravation and Fire.' It is interesting to see from the records that there were 46 pairs listed for this duty, which included 17 women. The women were sometimes paired together, but more often with a male colleague.

The first police station in Dulverton was built in 1858 on a site formerly occupied by a house and shop known as 'Bastille' and 'Caroline'. In 1902, this building was converted into a bank and at the time of writing, in 2002, is used as the Dulverton Pharmacy.

In 1867 there were bread riots throughout the country. In November, rumours were spread by 'mischiefmakers' that unless the baker reduced the price of a 4lb loaf there would be a riot in Dulverton and people would come in from the surrounding areas. This so alarmed the baker that he displayed a notice reducing the price from 8d. to $7^1/_2$d. When the day arrived the shops closed early and were guarded by police.

A rather less serious case was reported in 1887, when it was brought before the Petty Sessions:

Robert Cording, labourer, of Dulverton, was summoned for obstructing the highway in High-Street on June 2nd. P.S. Stark proved that a Miss Vickery had to go off the pavement, the defendant declining to move out of the way. Defendant was fined 1s. and 6d. costs. The money was paid.

In 1901, when larger premises were needed, the old Police Station was sold to a local builder, George Bowbeer Fisher, for £225, and a plot of land bought in Lady Street for £100. A new Police Station and court-house on the Lady Street site, costing £2,360, was agreed with a Taunton builder, Henry James Spiller, to be completed by 1902.

The earliest recorded names of local constables for Dulverton in 1861 were those of Messrs Henry Saunders, Henry Quick, John Fry and William Stone, and for Brushford: James Pine and George Blackmore.

Dulverton Police Station, 1970s.

In 1861, the total number of constables covering the parishes of Dulverton, Brushford, Hawkridge, Brompton Regis, Skilgate and Upton was 15. In 1993, there were three officers based at Dulverton: Sgt Morley Varker and PCs Dave Perry and Tony Rapson, and, by 1994, that number had dwindled to one. Dave Perry was the last to leave on 12 January 1994. At the time of writing, PC Colin Haddrell, our local policeman, shares the office with PC Pete Hopkinson who covers the Exford/Winsford area, while Mrs Fleur Blackmore keeps the office open five days a week for the Council Information Centre.

Other officers who served in Dulverton were: Sgt Bull, Sgt Russell, Jack Pullen, Bill Bird, Sam Udal, PC Partington, Len Trott, Tom Truman, Ron Stock, Ron Lavis, Sgt Tony Bell and Sgt Dave Osborne.

Most parishes had two constables who would have patrolled on foot – or possibly on horseback in this area. In 1861, the Chief Constable of Somerset was given 18 bicycles for use by his officers. It is not known if any found their way to Dulverton although it is possible that the superintendent for Dulverton, who lived at Wiveliscombe, may have been given one.

For many years, officers used to patrol their beats by visiting various 'points'. They were usually road junctions where there was a public phone box or a place with a phone, which the officers used to contact the station and send or receive messages, for many years reaching these points by bicycle, covering considerable distances in all conditions to get to them.

Around 1946 Dulverton had its first police car, a black Ford Prefect. Up until that point, they had only been used by senior officers. Apparently, it was kept immaculately clean to begin with as it was not known what to do with it. It was soon put to use as a taxi after pub closing time. It was also used to take young Geoff Udall (son of Sam Udall) to school. Geoff later joined the force and became a detective sergeant at Taunton.

Several stories are told about the police officers who covered Dulverton. In the early days there was a Sgt Bull who objected to the Carnival, the 'roll a penny' and other activities and the fireworks afterwards. As a result, on carnival night he was dangled off the bridge by locals who threatened to throw him into the Barle. When he returned to the town he was pelted with eggs. The eggs are purported to have been supplied by Miss Abbott – one of Dulverton's wealthy residents, indicating his unpopularity with all sections of the community. He left soon after this incident.

Sgt Len Trott was here in the 1960s, together with Constables Tom Truman and Ron Stock. Len was a very enthusiastic hunt supporter who was once driving along in his blue Ford by the side of the Barle with Mike Gammon, when they saw a stag running along the river. He stopped the car in the middle of the road, leapt out, leaving the door wide open, and ran off after the stag, with the local hunt coming along behind.

Len once wanted a salmon for the Superintendent but didn't know where to get one. He had been taught to fish by a local who knew exactly where to get one, and how. The trouble was that the method – using worms – was at that time unlawful. The local water bailiff, Bungy Williams, was ever vigilant. The Superintendent got his salmon!

PC Ron Lavis moved into Dulverton when they sold the police house at Brompton Regis in the early 1970s. He had a Triumph motor bike, which he used in his attempts to catch a certain poacher who targeted the Pixton Estate, among other places. Ron never caught him but he certainly kept him on his toes. He once remarked, 'every time I look in the mirror, I see Ron Lavis' motor bike.'

There was a local ritual involving after-hours drinking at the New Inn in the High Street (now Trumpington House Surgery). PC Bill Sparks and PC Jimmy Short used to ride their bikes through the town after closing time and park at the bottom of the High Street, walking up towards the New Inn. The late-night drinkers, having heard the motor bikes, would leave the bar and go outside to the back of the premises, just as Bill and Jimmy went in through the front door. After their inspection Bill and Jimmy would leave the New Inn and walk up the road to the Rock Inn, watched by the drinkers in the alleyway. It was then safe for them to re-enter the bar and carry on drinking.

The present Police Station in Exmoor Gardens was built in 1972 as were the three police houses opposite, which are now privately owned. The name 'Exmoor Gardens' was suggested by Mrs Mary Bell, wife of Sgt Tony Bell, who objected to the name 'Police House'. She said to the Chief Constable, Ken Steel, 'It was originally an allotment – why not Exmoor Gardens?' and so it has remained.

THE FIRE SERVICE

In January 1732, a meeting of the Town Trustees at the White Hart determined:

... that a fire engine be bought for the use of this town according to the agreement formerly made and subscribed by the majority of the Good men of this Town and now confirmed.

In 1739, a fire engine and 12 buckets were purchased and are believed to have been housed behind Bilbao House. In 1746, E.D. Graddon was paid 5s. per annum to clean and maintain the engine, keeping it well oiled (buckets and hoses were made of leather). In 1778, a new engine was purchased at a cost of £22.

Dulverton Fire Squad in their new uniforms, 2000. Left to right, standing: *Martin Snell, Jon Snell, Colin Green, Station Officer Ric Stanbury, Ken Paviour, Charles Buckingham, Steve How, Keith Williams;* seated: *Martin Waterman, Mark Hooper, Frank Gabb, Dave Thomas.*

Above and right: *The fire at Ellertons, Dulverton, 1922.*

Below: *Ready to go home, the Exeter Fire Brigade, 1922. The man with the cigarette is Walter John Steer.*

Dulverton Fire Brigade

Standing-down parade, Dulverton National Fire Service (including seven ladies), c.1946.

Demolition day at the Old Fire Station, 1986.

The Old Fire Station, Lady Street, after the fire, 1986.

Dulverton Firemen, late 1960s. Left to right, back: Fred Wilson, Fred Chanter, Fred Hodges, Norman Goss, Jim Herniman, Jack Hayes, Fred Hawkins, Roy Cross, Eric Coombs, Art Chanter; front: John Stanbury, ?, ?, Wilfred Bellamy.

Dulverton Fire Brigade, 1972, at the time when the Old Fire Station was being decommissioned and the new one opened. Left to right, standing: *Jim Herniman, Jack Hayes, Dick Puttock, Fred Hawkins, Ivan Hooper, Tony Snell, Norman Goss, Fred Hodges, Roy Cross;* seated: *Eric Coombes, Chief Fire Officer Bulliou, Art Chanter, Fred Wilson.*

In 1853, the Town Trustees were advised to purchase an insurance policy for the town against fire for £400 and that 18s. was required to 'advertise tolls and conditions to let' for businesses or householders who wished to participate.

In 1867 the Globe Insurance Company – now the Liverpool and London Insurance Company – were asked to remove the engine from the Trustees' property – the Town Hall. The insurers replied to the effect that if the Trustees did not provide accommodation rent free, they would remove the engine from the town. The Old Red Lion stables in Cross Street (now Union Street) were then used.

In 1886 the Market House was used for the fire engine, which by 1922 was housed in Lady Street. L.G. Sloman, who was born at No.2 Chapel Street in 1914, remembers the Fire Brigade's equipment in the 1920s:

This consisted of a contraption difficult to describe. Basically it was a pump manned by four strong men on each side, pumping via a long pole. The jet of water so produced could cope with small fires, and of course Bampton and Tiverton Fire Brigades were always available for help. However, they could not manage

when a row of cottages by Barle Bridge caught fire and they were gutted.

Fred Wilson, who came to Dulverton in 1947, joined the Fire Brigade in 1949 and remained for 33 years. These are his taped recollections recorded in 1993:

It was based in Lady Street, Dulverton – we had call bells and sirens then. When we moved to the new Fire Station in Kemps Way, we had bleepers calling us out instead of the siren. There were many improvements, including the rate of communication. In the past any message we had to send to Taunton after an incident was sent by D.I. on a motorcycle, if they were just for information or whether they wanted extra fire engines for the job. Today they call up on the radio from the fire engine straight to Taunton. Chimney fires made up the biggest number of incidents, followed by heath and grass fires, particularly in the dry hot seasons we used to have years ago. Some years were very bad. One year we had to go to Minehead on Grabbist Hill, we were carrying water up to the top to put it round the water-tenders' wheels to stop them from burning, as the ground itself was on fire. Employers had to give permission to go, if the siren went, and to be off for quite long times.

One of the most memorable fires was when we went to Honeymead Farmhouse at Exford which was burned down and had to be rebuilt. In those days, we only had pumps with a limited amount of water on board. There was none at Honeymead that we could draw from and the water had to come up from Simonsbath, several miles away. The Fire Brigade used to meet once a week for a drill and, after it finished, we'd go into a pub for a drink, which was needed in the hot weather! We'd have an annual dinner in The Lion or The Lamb or The Rock.

Today the Fire Brigade is housed in Kemp's Way, having moved there in 1972.

From the start of the fire service in Dulverton to the present day, all firemen have been volunteers. The pictures show the strength of the Dulverton Fire Brigade in 2000, and their three vehicles. In 2002, we have special teams of 'Co-Responders' who are trained to offer basic life support. Funds for this were raised by the people of Dulverton and visitors through fêtes, carnivals, collections, raffles and also through private donations.

Laying the first sewers down Chapel Lane, after 1935.

PUBLIC WATER SUPPLY

The first pumps in the town were established in 1845 – one on the corner by the White Hart and another on the corner of what was Barrow & Chapman Solicitors' office, now Risden Hosegood. In 1924, with the agreement of Letitia Shoppee of Hollam House, the Dulverton Rural District Council put a culvert from the spring and ancient surface well at Rack Close into a water tank, for the purpose of supplying water to the town of Dulverton. This supply of water was dependent on a Council worker turning on the tap at 7 o'clock at night to fill up the tank and closing it again at 7 in the morning! L.G. Sloman remembers:

The toilet was in the corner of the back yard, back to back with next door's, an arrangement that understandably caused considerable embarrassment. No water was laid on, so it had to be fetched from a standpipe on the pavement down the road. Inevitably

this meant that there were always buckets of water standing around, adding to the chill.

What about baths? This was a weekly ritual via a large hip bath, in front of the fire of course. Finding enough hot water was a major task... and then there was the weekly wash; how my mother ever coped is an abiding mystery.

Charlie Steer, born in Dulverton in 1911, worked as caretaker at Dulverton Middle School and also gave a graphic taped account of what it was like to live in a house without any running water:

We had no water and no sanitation indoors. We had to go to that stream I told you about – and outside the blacksmith's shop was a dipping place. We used to go to what we called the gutter to fetch our washing water and all that, and no sink or anything inside. You had to bring it all out again and tip it down somewhere outside. [For] the drinking water we used to have to go out to by the Rock corner, out the end of the lane, and turn a tap, you know, but that was public water, and get our pitcher of water for drinking. That went on for years, and in the winter-time, when it was frosty you used to have to take out some paper to unfreeze the tap, because that one used to keep freezing.

Prior to 1935, it is thought likely that a spring source in the Hollam Valley served Dulverton, while Brushford had no public mains supply up to that time, the village relying on private springs or wells. A reservoir was commissioned in 1935 and was situated in the Hollam Valley, about half a mile above Town Marsh. The water came from a spring source on the edge of South Hill Common and, before being piped to the reservoir, was treated with chlorine and other chemicals at a small building below Northcombe Farm. Most of the chemicals had to be delivered manually as the ground around the building was so steep that it was accessible only by a farm tractor in good weather! From the reservoir, water was piped to Dulverton, Brushford and Exebridge. A supplementary supply in the Hollam Valley – from shallow spring sources – fed into a small underground reservoir which served the Amory Road and Barnsclose estates and some properties in Jury Road. This supply received no chlorination or other treatment.

During the 1950s, as houses were modernised, bathrooms installed and washing machines purchased, the demand for mains water increased dramatically, outstripping the capacity to provide sufficient water from existing sources. The supply was augmented in 1958 by the provision of a pumping station at Marsh Bridge with electric pumps extracting water from the River Barle, to be pumped to a treatment plant at Northcombe. Charlie Steer has memories of some of these events:

All down through the Hollam valley, there used to be quite a big stream. When we were children we used to go up there catching what we used to call Tommy Badlegs and put them in jars. After several years Dulverton got a bit short of water and of course they went up there, the valley, and took in quite a lot of it, so there wasn't so much coming down.

The local sources were abandoned when Wimbleball was opened around 1979 and Dulverton is now supplied from a service reservoir on Bury Hill.

As a postscript, it must be noted that Wimbleball was not greeted with undiluted pleasure in Bury itself. An item in the *Western Daily Press* reported a victory celebration by the residents of Bury who refused to give up their local supply of spring water in order to connect to the mains – even though they were told that the water was sometimes contaminated. Lieutenant Colonel Eric Dolman had lead the fight:

The situation is ridiculous. We are quite happy with the water we get now and we certainly don't want to change, while Mrs Nellie Hill, a farmer's wife said: 'I've drunk it for years and it hasn't done me any harm.'

PUBLIC-SECTOR HOUSING

After the First World War, Dulverton Rural District Council – like all local authorities – was required to provide 'housing for the working classes' under the Housing Acts of 1919 and 1924.

Battleton was the first development in the mid 1920s, consisting of twelve three-bedroom houses in all: two blocks of three, one block of four and a pair of semis.

In the mid 1930s, further houses were provided at the rear of the Bridge Inn, and some in Jury Road, following the demolition of many sub-standard

At least two generations of the Herniman family, at the Castle, 1914/18.

Frank Herniman with Marjorie Herniman on his knee, 1918/19.

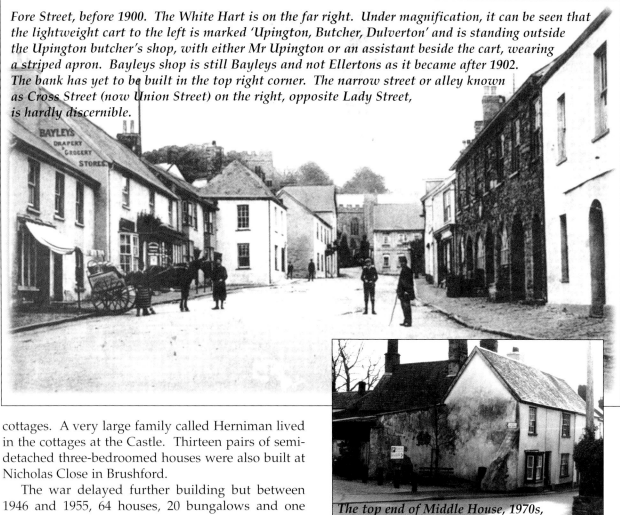

Fore Street, before 1900. The White Hart is on the far right. Under magnification, it can be seen that the lightweight cart to the left is marked 'Upington, Butcher, Dulverton' and is standing outside the Upington butcher's shop, with either Mr Upington or an assistant beside the cart, wearing a striped apron. Bayleys shop is still Bayleys and not Ellertons as it became after 1902. The bank has yet to be built in the top right corner. The narrow street or alley known as Cross Street (now Union Street) on the right, opposite Lady Street, is hardly discernible.

The top end of Middle House, 1970s, when the car park was created.

cottages. A very large family called Herniman lived in the cottages at the Castle. Thirteen pairs of semi-detached three-bedroomed houses were also built at Nicholas Close in Brushford.

The war delayed further building but between 1946 and 1955, 64 houses, 20 bungalows and one shop with a flat above were constructed on the Amory Road and Barnsclose estates. The shop eventually succumbed to competition from supermarkets and was turned into two separate flats. Six pairs of three-bedroom semis and three pairs of two-bedroom bungalows were built at Poundsclose, Brushford.

In the 1950s, the Government launched a scheme to provide small units of accommodation – with a warden service – for elderly people. Chypleys was the first scheme in Somerset, with eight one-bedroom units, and the first warden appointed was Mrs Bobbie Cornell.

Between 1960 and 1990, there was further development at Pixton Way, Fishers Mead and Barnsclose Mead, including four one-bedroom units as an extension of the Chypleys scheme. At Brushford, eight bungalows were built at Market Close.

The Government's 'Right to Buy' policy in 1981 resulted in many houses being sold under this scheme. Those remaining were sold by the local authority – by now the West Somerset District Council – to the Magna Housing Association in 1999.

In 1995, Local Authority involvement in the provision of publicly-owned rented accommodation ended with the transfer of their role to Housing Associations.

DULVERTON'S PUBLIC CAR PARKS

Less than 40 years ago there was no 'off-street' public car parking in the Dulverton area. It was also an offence to park on the road at night without lights. This was pretty strictly enforced by the local police force, headed in the 1960s by Sgt Trott and PC Tom Trueman of Dulverton. In any event, the battery power of most cars at that time prevented them from being parked with lights on for more than a few hours.

Mr Fred Wilson remembers the lack of cars. When interviewed in 1993 he said:

I've seen a great many changes. You'd see one or two tradesmen's vans, a few cars and taxis, although there were always charabanc or coach trippers. I've seen as many as 11 coaches in the town on one afternoon. Now of course it's more cars.

The increase in car ownership in the early 1960s highlighted the need for some off-street parking. The single vehicle driveway from the back of the Bridge Inn past Exmoor House to The Gardens was widened by filling in the ditch which separated it from the

◈ Road Improvements ◈

Above: *SCC Highways judging the roads at Dulverton.*

Right: *Cor! Look at our new tractor (the first one for the Dulverton Highways Department)! Left to right: Frank Collard, Les Stephens, Les Edmonds, Merv Chilcott, Tom Wood, Bill Tarr.*

Above left: *Congratulations after winning an award for road maintenance.*

Above: *The New Massey Harris Ferguson Tractor being inspected by the County judges.*

Left: *Dulverton Highway Department Best Maintenance Shield.*

Old Cottage opposite Battleton House before demolition, 1970.

It was demolished to allow motorists to see around the corner.

THE LIBRARY

The library began life as the Dulverton Club and Reading Room. In 1902, a public meeting was held in the Town Hall, chaired by Dr Sydenham, to institute a Working Men's Club. They decided on Mr Fisher's building in Lady Street. Rules were drawn up and a caretaker appointed.

The club offered bathroom facilities to everyone – locals to be charged 4d. for a hot bath and 2d. for a cold one, while visitors to the town were charged 6d. and 3d. respectively.

In 1903 a downstairs reading room was added, and newspapers such as the *Telegraph*, the *Mail*, the *Western Morning News* and magazines as varied as *Strand Magazine* and *Titbits* were provided. Old copies were later sold off to raise funds.

In the same year, Lady Margaret Herbert asked to hire the club for a Sewing Group at five shillings a session. Her request was originally granted but, in the following year, it was decided that the members did not want these women in their hallowed billiards room!

Over the years books were added to the reading material and it served as a library for the town until 1995/6, when it needed larger premises to cater for modern demands. It moved to the former German's Ironmongers, next to the Exmoor National Parks Visitors' Centre.

ELECTRICITY & TELEPHONE

Dulverton was one of the first small towns in England to have electricity. In September 1890, the Dulverton Improvement Association stated in their Annual Report that the town had been surveyed for electric lighting purposes. The Dulverton Electric Company was set up in 1905. Their power station was situated on the Barle at Battleton and can still be seen there.

Prior to that, George Fisher – that enterprising man – was creating sufficient electricity to light the Billiard Room and All Saints Church, though not both at the same time!

allotment land, and eight car spaces were provided. This was prior to the development of the Fire Station and the Police Station – at that time both still in Lady Street. Despite criticism that the spaces provided were 'a waste of public money by reason of the fact they were too far from the town', they were used and four more spaces added two years later.

Further developments took place in the former stable yard off the High Street, owned by the Lion Hotel. This was made possible by the widening of Union Street and the demolition of garage and workshop owned by G.C. Stanbury. At this time a footpath – to be named 'Abbots Way' – was constructed to link the town centre with Fishers Mead, Amory Road and Barnsclose. Before this, residents had to go around Jury Road, or take the safer but longer route via Millhams Lane and Chapel Street.

Additional parking was found when the allotment lands were developed. The Exmoor House car park was provided and later the Guildhall car park.

At one time, Mr John Organ tells us that in a search for suitable sites, consideration was given to developing land for parking on the far side of the River Barle from Exmoor House Lawns. This would either have meant visitors crossing the Town Bridge to get to the town, or the Council constructing a footbridge to meet the safety problem. This was considered too costly and the scheme was abandoned.

L.G. Sloman remembers when houses were being wired up at a standard fee of 1s.6d. per week. For this, he says, 'you could have two lights illuminated downstairs but, if a light was switched on upstairs, one downstairs light went off!'

Rigging the first telephone wires to go across Exmoor (no hard hats or harnesses – quite a feat of acrobatics).

My dear Mary & Sarah

I received your orders, but for the same reasons that I have stated in Fathers Letter it is impossible for me to execute them until the first week in December, I think I have stated to you before, that November is the busiest month in the year in this office, & it is impossible for me to leave the office to transact any business for myself — therefore bear this in your mind another time, the things you should have — when I sent the last parcel. You have not stated if you rec'd that parcel, nor the Hand sent by Alex — let me know if it was correct, & how you like them, & if you could contrive to furnish me with patterns of the colors you want, & the most ample description you can give me, for the taste as to these things in the Country is very different to the London taste.—

I don't exactly understand whether you mean Silk or Cotton Shawls which you call _____, describe them as well as you can —

If you have made any of my neck hand be so good as to send them when Alex — returns to Town, not cut in half —

Be pleased to give my love to all our Family & believe me to be your affectionate Bro

Geo Bryant

Letter from G. Bryant, sent by Pony Express in 1826.

THE POST OFFICE

The first mention of postage stamps in Dulverton was in 1856 and it is therefore likely that a Sub-Post-Office had been established in Dulverton by that time. Prior to that, it was all sealing wax and Pony Express! The first Sub-Postmaster was a Mr Catford who was also a herbalist and grocer. His shop was in what is now known as Governor House, next to Castlemoor.

After many years, probably in the early 1900s, the Telephone Exchange and Post Office was established on the corner of Lady Street, formerly Lock's Saddlery. An item in the *Free Press* of 5 September 1896 records:

A letter was read at Dulverton Parish Council from the Postmaster General in response to a petition for an evening delivery. The request was turned down on the grounds of insufficient correspondence.

Right: *PO staff, 1948.*
Left to right: *Olive Brodby and Hazeleen Foskett (telephonists), Bertha Lynch (telephonist supervisor), Barbara Hall (PO counter);* front: *John Stanbury's dog.*

Top: *Town Council, 1998/99 outside Exmoor House. Left to right, back: F.B. How, A. Crook;* middle: *M. Gammon, K. Ross, J. Luke, C. Gardiner, C. Nelder, R. Strutt;* seated: *P. Becker, P. Skipper, M. Balsom, T. Troake (Clerk), L. Stenner.*

This image: *Dulverton RDC staff on the occasion of the retirement of Mr Frank Herniman (Foreman, Manual Staff), 29 March 1963.* Left to right: *Griff Jones, Mildred Davenport, Cllr Ivan Kemp (Chair), Jack Parfitt, John Bennett, Mons Trelford, Alec White, Frank Herniman, George Bailey, Bert Matthews, Fred Hodge, Alfie Balsom, John Organ.*

THE TOWN COUNCIL

County Councils were created in 1848 and District Councils in 1894. Dulverton Parish Council had the responsibility of looking after and maintaining roads, drains, water, electricity, etc. Council meetings could range from the lively to the mundane. On 7 May 1921:

... plans to extend a charabanc service to Dulverton met stiff opposition. The council threatened to close the road and Miss E.M. Bent, who delivered milk along the route, said she could face storm and tempest but not Messrs Hardy's diabolical conveyances.

On 12 January 1946 the following was printed:

Dulverton RDC sanitary inspector reported that one ton of paper, 18 cwt of baled tins, half a cwt of rags and one cwt of bones had been collected in the past month.

One of the most memorable Council members was Ivan Jessie Kemp, who has Kemp's Way named after him.

Dulverton Players, Little Red Riding Hood, *1955.*

Dulverton Players, Monday Next, *April 1982.* Left to right: *Simon de Burgh, A. Rose, S. Summers, J. Heath, I. Baird, N. Mackney, K. Ross, Di Harding, C. Baird, B. Abbott.*

THIRTEEN

❧❧❧

STAGE & SCREEN

Organised public entertainment was almost non-existent until the turn of the 1900s. Drama was found in the rituals of daily life; the hunt, the kill, and the animals stampeding through the town. Farmers and their workers had the seasonal ordeals; the calving, lambing and the constant threat from predators. Hours were long and equipment was primitive, so it was quite a leap of faith that persuaded a group of enthusiasts to give Dulverton its own theatrical vehicle. This small but motivated group became known as the Dulverton Amateurs. Plays were produced before and after the First World War, to small but appreciative audiences. The sadness that lay over the country at the loss of the cream of its manhood was almost tangible and, with their productions, the Amateurs helped ease the grief of the local bereaved. These actors set a high standard too and, in 1927, they became known as the Dulverton Players; the 'company' which celebrated its 75th anniversary in 2002. Style and standard – a high standard – are the qualities that have remained unchanged over all those years, with the Players continually performing to a near professional level.

Very quickly, a schedule of two plays a year, in spring and autumn, was established. The challenge of television was met with relish and ingenuity, which was to stimulate rather than stifle amateur theatre. In recent years, sometimes four shows have been presented, each usually running for six performances. The relatively small stage in the Town Hall demands excellent sets, technical wizardry, good acting and astute directing.

The Players' successes include *Oh, What a Lovely War*, *The Sound of Music*, *A Man for All Seasons* and an open-air *Midsummer Night's Dream*; works ranging from Shakespeare to Sheridan, Oscar Wilde and Shaw to Ayckbourn, Stoppard and Arthur Miller. The Players' influence is felt in many areas throughout Dulverton; the former Pantomime Society merged with its theatrical big brother in 1972, which widened activities and encouraged hidden talents. Some pantomimes were staged at the Middle School to help school funds, and the Players still share equipment and expertise with the school and Youth Theatre activities.

In the relatively short space of 75 years, the Players have grown from a fledgling into a giant of the West, in terms of achievement and reputation. Their home, the Town Hall, has been transformed – it now has full catering facilities and a lift for wheelchair users, and even more modifications are scheduled.

Some 72 years ago, the *West Somerset Free Press*, in reviewing the farce, *Jane*, commented:

Dulverton at present has no clearly defined Amateur Dramatic Society or kindred organisation, but that there is plenty of room for one will not now be denied... it is to be hoped that steps towards such a body will be taken ere long.

They were!

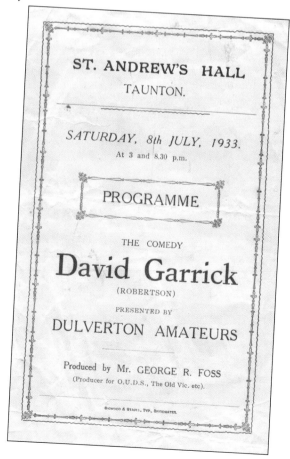

The Land Girls

Left: *Catherine McCormack being made up.*

Below left: *Filming on the Town Hall steps.*

Below right: *Extras playing Home Guard members and RAF personnel.*

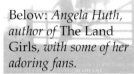

Below: *Angela Huth, author of* The Land Girls, *with some of her adoring fans.*

The three girls and the collie! **Left to right:** *Anna Friel played Prue, Rachel Weisz was Ag and Catherine McCormack played Stella.*

Location, location, location! This is the estate agent's legend for selling a house. And one which is also vital for making a film as evocative as *The Land Girls*, which was filmed in Dulverton and Bampton in 1997, with the whole-hearted support (and not a few extras) of the Dulverton Players. In fact, for the week or so of location filming in March of that year, it seemed that just about everyone in Dulverton was in uniform, Second World War vintage, of some description. Dulverton was given a makeover so that it resembled the town as it might have been in 1941, and it was so realistic that one or two real Land Army girls still living in the area were overcome with emotion.

In a wartime special issue, the *Mid Devon Gazette* quite accurately described Dulverton as being in 'a 1940s time warp'. Reporter John Nash wrote:

The distinctive snarl of a Spitfire engine lifted scores of heads to the skies. Soon, the rumble of ageing trucks echoed in the war-drab town streets and began to fill the air... Britain under siege 1941? No, peacetime Dulverton, 1997, as Greenpoint Films came to town... the area was transformed into one gigantic wartime set. 'It's the biggest thing to happen here since the War!' said a man outside the Town Hall.

The Land Girls brought world-wide fame to Dulverton for a few months; it was released nationally and overseas and the video proved a big seller, many being sent to relatives of Dulvertonians all over the world.

The film deals with three girls from different backgrounds who are sent to work on a West-Country farm. Apart from the big media attention and film publicity, the economic impact of the location filming was immense. Producer Simon Relph had a budget of £5 million. He estimated that at least £500,000 was spent locally.

As a young woman, Betty German lived in the town, so filming proved a nostalgic time for her. In those days she lived in German's Cottages, now the home of the Heritage Centre. Betty said:

Life went on in spite of the war. We had lots of social evenings and dances, but they had to be over early because of the blackout. Everybody did things for the war effort and there were lots of Land Girls working on farms in the area.

Mrs Mary Atkins, 67, was dressed as an air-raid warden. She was evacuated to the town in 1942. Mary said, 'I have wonderful memories and how the town looks today is just how it was back then. There were a lot of Land Army girls then.' The filming put Dulverton on the world map for a time and the film company, Greenpoint, were delighted with the reception they received. Associate producer Andrew Warren wrote to the Town Council: 'Such an event could not have been possible without the total support of the town, and this we have certainly had.' With the letter came a cheque for £3,000, as a 'thank you' from the film-makers. Everyone in Dulverton really was a 'Player' during that week to remember.

∽ Armed Forces, early 1900s ∾

Royal 1st Devon Imperial Yeomanry, Ashwick, 1909.

Left: *Dulverton Platoon 1st North Devon Yeomanry. 3rd and 4th from right, kneeling: Walter J. Steer, Officer Lt Sowton Barrow; 6th from right, standing: Charles W. Steer (died 1904 after attending Army Camp).*

Yeomanry at Winsford Hill, 1909.

FOURTEEN

❧❧

THE ARMED FORCES

THE ARMY

Local records show that Dulverton men have served in the Army since 1774, all in Foot Regiments, some for 30 years or more. In 1804, records show that the Dulverton Volunteers consisted of 114 privates, 5 sergeants and 1 commandant, and that 44 of these men could not sign their names. By 1806, the number of privates had fallen to 95, the Napoleonic Wars having taken their toll.

By 1880, the North Devon Yeomanry together with, possibly, the West Somerset Yeomanry, was formed. Many Dulverton men served in the Armed Forces during the Boer War and the First and Second World Wars. In All Saints Church a tablet is displayed in memory of Trooper Simpson, formerly of Northmoor. It reads:

In 1900 he had volunteered for service in South Africa with other Dulverton yeomen. Of the four that went out, Sergeant A. Marshall, Corporal Bawden and Trooper Heywood returned unscathed after suffering many hardships, but Trooper Simpson died of enteric fever in the field hospital at Thorndale. He had been with General Rundle in the relief of Wepener, marched to Pretoria under Lord Roberts, and fought at the battle of Diamond Hill.

One Dulvertonian, Bill Rendell, recorded his recollections and memories, including his time in the Army during the First World War: the early days at Gallipoli; the appalling conditions and their effect on the men; and of being sent to hospital in Egypt, home to England to recuperate, and then back again to Egypt. He was part of the Lawrence of Arabia campaign, eventually ending the war at the Front Line in France, shortly before the Armistice. At the outbreak of the Second World War, Bill became a Special Constable.

The film *The Land Girls* gives a flavour of Dulverton during the war years (see Chapter Thirteen). Despite the sadness, hard work and wartime deprivations, there was also excitement as the town was caught up in the feverish activity and changes brought about by war.

A number of American soldiers were stationed here from March to June 1944. One of them, Marven McCain of Panama City, Florida visited the Heritage Centre in 1995. He told how they detrained at Dulverton Station and marched with all their kit up to Haddon where they camped. The only vehicles they had which could get around our narrow roads were jeeps, but these were frequently wrecked as their drivers failed to negotiate a bend. In fact, he says, more men were killed in the months when they were here than his unit lost on D-Day! He also recalled that the pretty daughter of the landlord of the Lion was being lusted after by two of his senior officers – one a colonel, the other a mere lieutenant colonel – and that the more senior officer frequently pulled strings to keep the other in camp, much to the amusement of the enlisted men.

Lion Menu card signed by American soldiers who came down from Haddon Camp, May 1944. It includes some fictional names!

Soldiers hitching the horses to the gun carriage by the Lion Inn, 1909.

Outside the Lion Inn/Woods Café; soldiers displaying their armoury to the local boys, 1909.

request to keep her on as housekeeper at Highnam Farm, and Jean joined the Navy, in which her brother also served. She worked for three years at the Royal Navy Hospital, Plymouth as a Grade 1 nurse and remembers going on the wards or to lectures in a gas mask or hard hat, and also working at Plymouth Dockyards. It was at the hospital that she met and married her husband, both of them eventually returning to Dulverton.

RAF

Over the years several planes have crashed on the high ground around Dulverton. Ken Phillott remembers an incident before the war:

In 1930, Captain Popkiss, owner of the Lion Hotel, had a friend who was the pilot of the R100 and he got him to fly over Dulverton. Unfortunately, at the time it was very foggy so that we could only hear the drone of the engines. Even so, 'Postie' Puttock waved his postbag and shouted 'Yer's Dulverton!'... the airship eventually crashed and became a burned out wreck.

During the war, as there was no airfield, searchlights were placed around the town. In spite of this, a B17 Flying Fortress crashed on 20 March 1944 whilst returning home from a bombing raid on Frankfurt.

Above: *The Lion Hotel, early 1940s (?).*

Left: *Jean Campbell, a Red Cross nurse in the Royal Navy Hospital at Plymouth, 1943.*

THE NAVY

The first record we have of a naval link with the town is of George Lewis Browne, who was born in Dulverton in 1784 and died in Bristol around 1856. Lt Browne served with Lord Nelson at Trafalgar and is said to have been the officer who raised Nelson's famous signal, 'England Expects... ' in 1805.

In 1941 Dulverton and district raised £71,000 in War Weapons Week. By March 1942, they had raised a further £52,931, just £2,000 short of their target for Warship Week. The town's ambition to adopt the destroyer HMS *Dulverton* was realised. Sadly, in November 1943, the ship was sunk whilst in action in the Aegean Sea. Five medals were awarded for bravery, two posthumously. The present ship's company has visited Dulverton on several occasions.

Many young Dulvertonians have joined the Navy, including Marian Diane Campbell (née Heywood) – always known as 'Jean'. Jean Campbell received her call-up papers while working at The Retreat – now the Youth Hostel next to the Catholic Church – which, at the time, was being used as a sick bay for evacuees. The authorities turned down her father's

Top: *Debris retrieved in 2001 from a Flying Fortress which crashed on Court Down on 20 March 1944.*
Above: *Two local lads who served in the Royal Air Force, Second World War. Left is Richard 'Dick' Steer, right is 'Paddy' Kennedy. They are pictured at RAF Locking, Weston-super-Mare.*

1st Battalion Scots Guards, 1949–50, showing John Ridler as goalkeeper.

13th Company Grenadier Guards, for whom four members of the Scots Guards were persuaded to play, 1949–50.   John Ridler is goalkeeper.

Home Guard outside Exmoor House, Section 1.

Home Guard outside Exmoor House, Section 2.

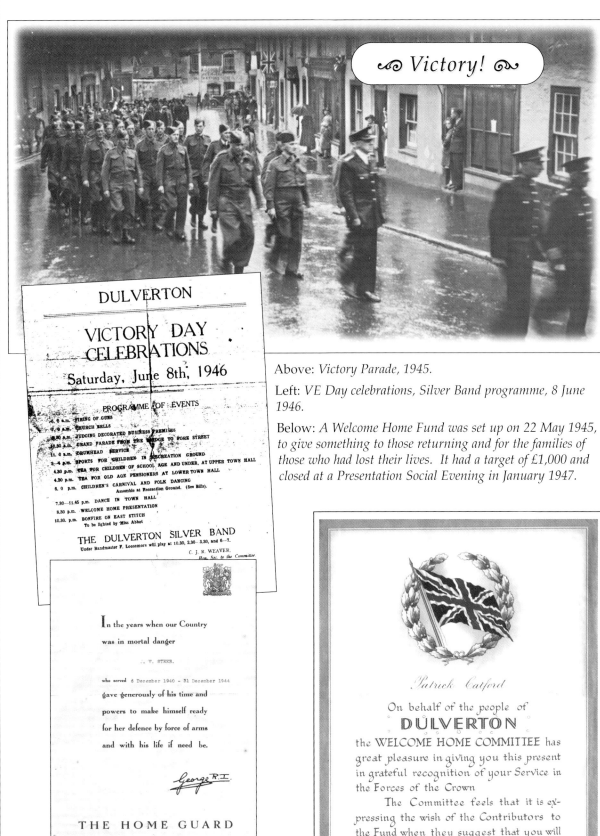

Victory!

DULVERTON

VICTORY DAY CELEBRATIONS

Saturday, June 8th, 1946

PROGRAMME OF EVENTS

6. 0 a.m. FIRING OF GUNS
7. 0 a.m. CHURCH BELLS
9.30 a.m. JUDGING DECORATED BUSINESS PREMISES
10.30 a.m. GRAND PARADE FROM THE BRIDGE TO FORE STREET
11. 0 a.m. DRUMHEAD SERVICE
2—4 p.m. SPORTS FOR CHILDREN IN RECREATION GROUND
4.30 p.m. TEA FOR CHILDREN OF SCHOOL AGE AND UNDER, AT UPPER TOWN HALL
4.30 p.m. TEA FOR OLD AGE PENSIONERS AT LOWER TOWN HALL
6. 0 p.m. CHILDREN'S CARNIVAL AND FOLK DANCING
          Assemble at Recreation Ground. (See Bills).
7.30—11.45 p.m. DANCE IN TOWN HALL
8.30 p.m. WELCOME HOME PRESENTATION
10.30 p.m. BONFIRE ON EAST STITCH
           To be lighted by Miss Abbot

THE DULVERTON SILVER BAND
Under Bandmaster F. Loosemore will play at 10.30, 2.30—3.30, and 6—7.

C. J. R. WEAVER,
Hon. Sec. to the Committee

Above: *Victory Parade, 1945.*

Left: *VE Day celebrations, Silver Band programme, 8 June 1946.*

Below: *A Welcome Home Fund was set up on 22 May 1945, to give something to those returning and for the families of those who had lost their lives. It had a target of £1,000 and closed at a Presentation Social Evening in January 1947.*

In the years when our Country

was in mortal danger

... W. STEER.

who served 6 December 1940 – 31 December 1944

gave generously of his time and

powers to make himself ready

for her defence by force of arms

and with his life if need be.

George R.I.

THE HOME GUARD

Many local men were in reserved occupations and therefore served in the Home Guard. They all received certificates acknowledging their service to the country and marched through the town on the Victory Day celebrations.

Patrick Catford

On behalf of the people of
DULVERTON
the WELCOME HOME COMMITTEE has great pleasure in giving you this present in grateful recognition of your Service in the Forces of the Crown

The Committee feels that it is expressing the wish of the Contributors to the Fund when they suggest that you will buy something with it which will be a lasting reminder to you and your Family of your War Service

FIFTEEN

୧ଏ⊙ଚ

DULVERTON'S CHURCHES

ALL SAINTS, DULVERTON

For centuries, the Parish Church has been the focus of the English village. All Saints, on its hillside, both overlooks the town and can be seen from everywhere within it. Folk go about their business with half an eye to the cross of St George proudly flying from the thirteenth-century tower, or half an ear to the fine peel of bells, the earliest dating from the sixteenth century and the latest from 1907, still regularly rung. First the snowdrops, then the crocuses and finally the daffodils cheer all who pass the churchyard in the first months of each year. Although we cannot be sure, there has probably been a church on the present site since early-Saxon times and an ancient burial-ground will almost certainly pre-date the first church.

The history of the church is hazy until the time of the Norman Conquest. Richard de Turberville, who held the manor by gift of Henry I, gave the church and land around it to the Augustinian Priory at Taunton in 1130.

Lychgate, All Saints, Dulverton.

Some 50 years later, the Augustinians established St Nicholas' Priory at Barlynch on the banks of the Exe to the north-east of the town. The canons held the living until the Dissolution during the reign of King Henry VIII, when it was given to the Earl of Oxford. Indeed, from 1338, the priory possessed the manor and hundred of Dulverton as well. Today all that remains of Barlynch, which was a small priory, are stones in the farmhouse of that name and, perhaps, the oldest bell in All Saints. There is a complete record of vicars from 1332 to the present day, 53 of them altogether, with an early vacancy sadly caused by the Black Death.

The present church, apart from the tower, dates from the mid-nineteenth century. By then the building, erected around the end of the fifteenth and start of the sixteenth century, was in need of repair. England was prosperous in the 1850s and there was the means to match the need – perhaps too much so, because the architect, Mr Ashworth, was able to rebuild the church completely, doing nothing to save any of the fittings of the old church including a fine rood-screen. Even so, the Victorians displayed typical prudence and thrift. The building contract stipulated that the contractor should 'not on any account or pretence exceed the sum of two thousand and five hundred pounds'!

The church is well loved and well cared for as witnessed by the exceptionally fine set of kneelers, each one different and depicting something relevant to church, town or Exmoor, and bearing the initials of its maker. Some of the windows commemorate local people of note: Henry John George, Third Earl of Carnarvon; Henrietta Anna, Countess Dowager of Carnarvon; George Williams, born at Ashway Farm and founder of the YMCA; and George Hall Peppin, born in the parish in 1800, who emigrated in 1850 from Old Shute Farm to Australia where he bred Merino sheep. His diary records opening a case of gin each month when he did his accounts! There are memorials to members of the Sydenham family and the tombstone of Dr Collyns, the renowned expert on red deer, can be found against the east wall of the church.

Revd James Philby (Vicar of Dulverton, 1892–1909) and family.

Main: *All Saints before 1895.*

Inset: *The incumbent at the time of writing, the Revd Anthony Appleby.*

Left: *Stump of 300-year-old sycamore tree in All Saints Churchyard, brought down in a storm during the 1970s.*

The Clock & Bell Tower

The tower is an original Norman structure with later modifications. The clock was installed in 1708 and for close on 200 years had a delightful chime which to the town and people said:

*Old John Wesley's
dead and gone
He left us in the tower,
'Twas his desire that we should play
At Eight and Twelve and Vower.*

In 1887, the old chimes were replaced by new ones – those we hear today. This venerable clock now has a team of minders and winders, all of whom, when their turn comes around, stagger up a well-worn, narrow Norman staircase to the clock chamber to wind the clock – a very physical effort! Each member of the team winds for seven days every six weeks. They are: Derek Peck, David Lloyd, John Page, Peter Loweth, John Burton, Ron Massie and his faithful assistant, Tizzie (by kind permission of the Rector).

The bells of All Saints are as follows:

Bell	Maker	Year	Weight
Treble	John Taylor, Loughborough	1907	4.1.1.
Second	John Taylor	1907	4.0.18.
Third	John Taylor	1884	4.3.20.
Fourth	Thomas Pennington	1619	5.1.21.
Fifth	Thomas Pennington	1640	7.1.25.
Sixth	Thomas Pennington	----	7.3.19.
Seventh	Exeter Foundry	1500s	11.2.0.
Tenor	Thomas Pennington	----	13.0.12.

(Information kindly supplied by John Taylor Bellfounders Ltd)

The ringers as at September 2001 were: Jim Walker (Tower Captain), Michael Browring, Mike Cummins, Jane Lindsay, Peter Loweth, Mary-Ann Marlow, Barry Nixon, Rod Strutt and Paddy Tuckett.

Chapel of Ease

A chapel of ease was built close to Marsh Bridge by Arthur Locke in the late-nineteenth century. There are photographs, but nothing of the chapel now remains.

Northmoor Chapel at Marsh Bridge, c.1900. Northmoor House can be seen to the left (picture left).

SERVICES.

Sundays

8 a.m. Holy Communion.
11 a.m. Mattins, Litany and Sermon.
3 p.m. The Catechism.
6.30 p.m. Evensong and Sermon.

On the first Sunday in the month Litany is said at 7.45 a.m., and there is a second Celebration after Mattins.

Week Days
(except Mondays).

Mattins 8 a.m.
Evensong 6 p.m.
      Oct. to April.
7 p.m., May to Sep.
Litany at 12. Wednesday and Friday.

Saints' Days
H.C. 8.
Catechism 4.
Evensong 6.

Churchings
Before any Week Day Service.

Holy Baptism
At any Evensong or other time by arrangement.

Vicar:
Rev. H. J. Green, M.A., Oxon.
Churchwardens:
Mr. G. F. Sydenham, Mr. G. B. Fisher.
Sidesmen:
Messrs. J. Fry, W. Slade, G. Catford, W. A. Hawkins, G. H. Fisher, R. J. Collyns, H. A Noyes W. Beed.
Organist: Mr. H. Catford.
Sexton: Mr. T. Sayer

ARCH. LOCKE

IT IS REQUESTED THAT WORD BE SENT TO THE VICAR AT ONCE, IN ALL CASES OF SICKNESS.

∾ The Parish Magazine ∾

The Parish Magazine *is still published each month but in a different format. Unfortunately it is not known when it originated. By looking at this 1912 copy, only the two outer pages were printed in Dulverton, containing all of the church information and local advertisements, etc. The centre pages appear to have been printed in London in a magazine form called* The Signs.

Left: *A wedding at All Saints Church. From left: Gilbert Sparks, Jean Sparks, Elsie Sparks, Alan Steer (best man), Derek Sparks (groom), Kathleen Hall (bride), Ivor Hall, Jean Hall, Mrs Hall.*

Below: *All Saints Church Choir, 1933/34. From left, back: Mrs Stanbury, ?, Ken Chilcott, Charley Burton, Revd and Mrs Ludlow and daughter, Joe How, ? Parkhouse, R. Herniman, Bill Greenslade, ? Chilcott, Mr Weaver (choirmaster and headmaster); front: G. Stark, Joe Hancock, Sonnie Gammon, H. Stark, G. Crocker, Bert Cockram, John Hancock.*

Bottom: *All Saints Male Voice Choir, c.1910.*

The
❧ Chapel ❧
Community

Congregational Church group, late 1920s.

Congregational Church group, early 1900s.

Congregational Church group, July 1931.

THE CONGREGATIONAL CHURCH

After the Reformation, the Church of England was established by law as the only authorised Church. Catholics who stayed loyal to the old religion were persecuted, as were Nonconformists, or Independents as they were then called. They had to worship in secret or flee to other countries. There was a respite during Cromwell's Commonwealth, but in 1662, soon after the restoration of the monarchy, some 2,000 clergy of the established Church felt compelled to give up their living 'for fidelity to God and to conscience'. The dissenting churches date from this time. Many of their members supported the Monmouth Rebellion and, no doubt, there were men from Dulverton who heard Monmouth proclaimed King in Taunton on 18 June 1685 and followed him to eventual defeat at the Battle of Sedgemoor. The Toleration Act of 1689 allowed Nonconformists to gather in premises licensed by the bishop. That year, the house of John Crewe was licensed for preaching and, in 1710, the New Hall was built. There were 200 members of the meeting-house in its opening year, some of 'the first rank and fortune'.

Nonconformity in Dulverton was in decline by the start of the nineteenth century and meetings were again being held in the houses of individuals. In November 1830, the Revd Standerwick was appointed pastor and he at once made plans for a chapel. It was begun in 1831 and on completion was known as the Dulverton Independent Church – the church which we know today. The manse was added in 1887, thanks to the generosity of George Williams, and at the end of the century the flourishing Sunday School was provided with eight small classrooms. The Independent Congregational Church is still in good heart, its members quietly but effectively working hard for the benefit of their fellow townsfolk.

Above: *Congregational Church group members after Sunday Service, 1995.*

Right: *A group from the Congregational Church, 1970s.*

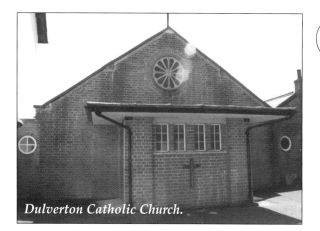

Dulverton Catholic Church.

Catholic Church

Above: *Mrs Aubrey Herbert, 1970s.*

Left: *Father Robert Miller with the High Sheriff of Somerset (Micaela Becket), Father Christmas (Richard Carr), and assistants Inigo and Theadora Barker* (left) *and Beatrice and Ester Watson* (right) *at the Christmas Bazaar, 1998.*

Father Robert Miller during a service, 1998.

The Methodist Church

Methodism grew out of the Church of England. Both John and Charles Wesley were Anglican ministers. Their elder brother Samuel was headmaster of Blundells and both visited the area. Records show that around 1810, Dulverton Methodists began meeting at the house of Mr Liscombe, a tanner, and over the years at other houses and cottages, but in 1826, most of the few Methodists joined the Congregational Church. Then, in 1852, a meeting-room was registered in the name of John Banwell, a Bible Christian minister of Kings Brompton. For a while, Methodists seem to have aroused opposition and meetings were sometimes disturbed by a mob gathering around the door. But as the century drew to its close, things looked up and, in 1902, a chapel was built in Lady Street. The cost of the site was £90 and the building was paid for by donations, fundraising efforts and two loans of £200 each from persons living at Sampford Peverell, at $3\frac{1}{2}$ per cent interest. Electricity was added in 1906 at a cost of £10 and a new organ installed in 1938 at a cost of £26. The chapel was converted into flats in the 1990s.

St Stanislaus Catholic Church

Mrs Aubrey Herbert was a Catholic and converted a corrugated-iron hut at Pixton Park into a chapel where Mass was celebrated once a month for the few Catholics in the town and neighbourhood. The Second World War saw an influx of Catholics; Polish soldiers and a convent school evacuated to Hollam House. Mrs Herbert looked for a site and persuaded her architect friend and visitor to Pixton, Sir Albert Richardson, President of the Royal Academy, to design a church. His sketch plan exists but the church does not. Rather than build a new church, the stables at the Retreat in Bridge Street were converted, the work being undertaken under the leadership of Father Whelan by local men including the Kennedy brothers, Edgar and Paddy, and Ron Mathews. The church was opened in 1955, its dedication to St Stanislaus of Cracow, the patron saint of Poland, the inspiration of Auberon Herbert who fought in the war with the Polish Army and devoted himself after the conflict to the resettlement of Polish servicemen unable to return to their country. A number of the church furnishings were originally in the chapel at Pixton, including the altar, with the Portuguese dossal behind it and a fine crucifix by Eric Gill. The two cartwheel windows were made at Buckfast Abbey and most of the original simple steel windows have been replaced with stained-glass windows. There are two paintings by Richard Rothwell, a local artist from Morebath, and a wooden statue of St George by Septimus Waugh, a local sculptor. The private house, the Retreat, was at first used as the presbytery but, since the 1980s, has been a residential youth centre for the Diocese of Clifton, much in demand by canoeists in the winter months.

Quakers

A meeting-house in Town Marsh – known as Marsh Hall – was built in the 1880s by the Mildmays for the Quakers. Will Steer put the roof on in 1884. This is now a private house.

A wedding group at the former Catholic Church at Pixton, 23 June 1931, gathered for the marriage of Ron Mathews and Margaret Malone. Father Whelan is on the far right.

St Nicholas Church, Brushford.

Brushford Church Flower Festival.

SIXTEEN

ᔡᔥᔤ

BRUSHFORD & EXEBRIDGE

BRUSHFORD

Collinson, in 1791, described Brushford as a 'pleasing situation two miles south east of Dulverton on the extreme edge of Somerset towards Devon', pointing out that 'the River Barle divides Brushford from Dulverton.' The name of Brushford derives from the faggots which were used to create a ford and bridge across the Brockeye, a small river which passes through the village. Collinson continues:

The situation of this place is pleasing, being on a declivity, surrounded by hills intersected with hedgerows and spotted with woods. Houses are 66 in number, which lie round the Church (St Nicholas) or are dispersed in the hamlets of Knightcot and Langridge. The latter is situated southward from the village and was formerly a considerable place, with a chapel and a Fair which is still held here in August. This manor of Langridge once belonged to the ancient family of Bretton.

The church of St Nicholas is a small fifteenth-century building with a strong well-built tower at the West end in which are five bells, built in the seventeenth century.

Various bequests of money recorded in the church show the interest to be used for the poor each Lady Day. The Charity Commissioners' Report of 1819/37 cites the John Norris Charity:

John Norris, clerk, by indenture, enrolled in the Court of Chancery and bearing the date 23 June 1742, gave seven pounds yearly, for ever, out of his estate of Langaller, in the parish, for teaching twenty poor

Left to right: *Jim Summers, Patrick Wood and Richard Hodge out shooting at Upcott, late 1920s.*

children to read, and to purchase books for such poor children.

According to the Report, this rent was paid regularly by the owner of Langaller estate and later by the steward of Lord Carnarvon, the then proprietor. We therefore suppose that a charity school existed in Brushford from the time of John Norris' bequest. The Report refers to two small schools in the parish which shared the annual sum between them: '... what is not expended in the purchase of books, is divided between the two schoolmistresses.'

Later records show that in 1822, Brushford contained 64 inhabited houses and 67 families, 54 of which were employed in agriculture.

In 1836 an endowed National School was built close to the church and was extended in 1892. Old Way End, Knightcott and Exebridge were hamlets of Brushford, with Exebridge connecting Somerset and Devon. The Post Office, however, was at Exebridge, not Brushford, with a Mrs Grace Tidball, as sub-Postmistress. Exebridge also had a miller at that time and there is a reference to the water-mill at Exebridge.

The records for 1872 stated: '... the Wesleyans have a place of Worship here', although it is not said where, and that the schoolmistress of the National School was a Mrs Mary Anne Kent. The railway station was in the process of development near Brushford and, three years later, Goodlands was established at the railway station.

By 1889 a toll-free monthly market was held on the first Tuesday in each month, close to the railway station; during the tourist season, a four-horse coach

Brushford School, 1912, taken in front of the school with the teacher, Miss Bishop, and children.

Brushford School, early 1920s, in the schoolroom.

Brushford School, a class of 1957.

Brushford School Juniors in the playground, 1957.
Left to right, back: *L. Chilcott, J. Taylor, M. Gurney, J. Bidgood, G. Fyfe, C. Tarr, D. Somerwill, J. Cook;*
middle: *J. Coggins, B. Wright, M. Perring, R. Rawle, P. Parfitt, M. Kinsman, C. Tout;*
front: *M. Bidgood, C. Hayes, J. Northcott, B. Cook, S. Robins, E. Watts, S. Perry, M. Vellacott, G. Newton.*

Thomas Troake

Above:
Tom Troake
(1920–2001).

Main: *'Penny Social' showing*
Tom Troake and others on 21 December
1986, raising funds for a new
Village Hall.

Tom Troake as a young soldier.

Certificate of Appreciation

From Dulverton Town Council
on behalf of the Community
to

Thomas Troake Esq

In gratitude for 15 years of
loyal service to the Town
Awarded on
31st March 2000

Signed P.E. Skipper.
Council Chairman.

E^{II}R

The Lord Chamberlain is
commanded by Her Majesty to invite

Mr. Thomas Troake
to a Garden Party
at Buckingham Palace
on Tuesday 13th July 1999 from 4 to 6 pm

This card does not admit

Left: *Buckingham*
Palace Garden Party
invitation addressed
to Tom Troake, 13
July 1999.

Far left: *Certificate*
of Appreciation from
Dulverton Town
Council to T. Troake,
31 March 2000.

left the Carnarvon Arms for Lynmouth on Tuesdays, Thursdays and Saturdays to meet the train which left London at 9.00am, and returned from Lynmouth on alternate days.

The old village hall at Brushford was demolished in the late eighties, Rosemary Hart and Ellen Maund having worked very hard to raise funds for a new one.

The Church of St Nicholas

The Vicar of Dulverton is also the Rector of St Nicholas, Brushford. The oldest part of the church is believed to be the south wall of the nave which may date from the thirteenth century. The two windows in this wall were inserted during the fifteenth century. The fine Perpendicular screen belongs to about the same period. There is a Norman font of Purbeck marble and some pews dating from Tudor times.

There are also twentieth-century features of note: the north chapel, erected in 1926 as a memorial to Aubrey Herbert, son of the 4th Earl of Carnarvon, MP for South Somerset and a great adventurer – who was the model for Buchan's 'Greenmantle' – was designed by Sir Edwin Lutyens; the effigy is by Cecil Howard; and there is also a memorial to Mrs Aubrey Herbert, the inscription on which is by Denis Tegetmeier, collaborator and son-in-law of Eric Gill.

Tom Troake (1920–2001)

Tom Troake played the organ at St Nicholas Church from the age of 16 until his death. He lived in Brushford for the greater part of his life and also played the organ in Dulverton and for numerous church choirs. In 1999 he was presented by the Archdeacon with the Diocesan Coat of Arms for his long service as organist – a very rare award.

In 1940, without waiting for his call-up papers, he left Barrow & Chapman, Solicitors, and volunteered for the Royal Army Pay Corp, serving with them for six years. After the war he ran the office at Dulverton Sawmills – later to become Exmoor Woodcraft – and then joined Radley & Chanter until his retirement.

Tom never liked being idle and, wondering what he was going to do in retirement, became Clerk to the Dulverton Town Council, holding this office for 15 years. During this time he was also a ward member of West Somerset District Council for a decade and Chairman of Brushford Parish Council. He belonged to Brushford Bowls Club, was a keen photographer and was founder member of Dulverton Camera Club. He was also responsible for the film of the Queen's Silver Jubilee celebrations at Brushford in 1977. At the age of 78 he enrolled on a computer course and passed all his exams with distinction. As the address at his funeral made clear, he was a 'truly remarkable man'.

Riphay Barton Orchard – these trees have now all gone.

Above:
*Brushford
Football Team,
season
1913–14.
Circled is the
team mascot.*

Left: *Bell-
ringers at
Brushford
Church, 1950.
Left to right:
Irene Wensley,
William Troake,
Revd John
Stubbs, Bert
Baker and
Gordon Hooper.*

Dulverton Home Guard – Brushford Group.
Middle row: *7th from left: Barry Hodge, Upcott Farm;* back row 2nd from right: *Bill Hayes, Higher Upcott.*

Brushford Land Army girls at Langaller, 1953.

Top: *Part of the 1953 Coronation celebrations at Brushford, outside the old Parish Hall.*

Above: *Brushford's balance sheet for the celebrations of the Coronation of King George V, 23 June 1911.*

Left: *Poster advertising the events to be staged for the occasion.*

EXEBRIDGE

Judging by *Kelly's Directory* of 1897 Exebridge had changed from being just a hamlet of Brushford and was by this time thriving separately on its own. It mentions: Will Bennett, Blacksmith; Bob Bishop, Mill Manager to Mr Francis Langdon (landowner); William Lock Gibbins, Wheelwright; John Pyke, Shoemaker; and Edgar Hill, Water Bailiff to the Exe Salmon Fishery Board.

In 1897, Francis Langdon – farmer and miller at Riphay Barton and Exebridge – had established the Exe Valley fish-breeding establishment. By 1902, Theo Fred Tracy had the Exe Valley Fishery and Thomas Culverwell Yandle was at Riphay, as farmer and miller. By 1906, the mill had passed into the hands of James Squire. In 1914, Exe Valley Fisheries were still owned by Mr Theo Tracy and the mill had disappeared. By 1919, Mrs Henrietta Pyke had opened a laundry at Exebridge.

Personal memories put some bones on these rather dry facts. Around 1900, Mr and Mrs Richard Radford moved from Bampton to Exebridge where they brought up their five children – four girls and a boy. Three of their grandchildren – Thelma and Ernest (Ivy's children) and Mollie (Violet's daughter) – have recalled and documented some of their memories of visits to Exebridge in the late 1920s to stay with their grandparents. Thelma remembers:

The journey to Exebridge from faraway places was quite an event for young children. Living near Nottingham, we would catch the Devonian express from Derby, then at Taunton we changed to the little Exe Valley train, single track to Dulverton. Waiting was Mr Takle with his taxi, a large sedan car with the hood folded back, showing the shiny leather upholstery. At the station, there was also a little 'square' bus with the sign 'The Lamb Hotel' on the front and by the door stood the driver, Dan, wearing a long white coat and a black shiny peaked cap, waiting for Dulverton passengers.

Mollie recalls:

As a small child, my visits to the countryside were idyllic and only later did I realise the hard lives the adults lived. At Dulverton Station we crossed the railway line to take a shortcut. Later this was stopped because someone was killed on the track. After that we had to go round by the bridge, walking the mile to Exebridge. When we got there, my mother would buy us two ounces of butterscotch sweets from the village Post Office, which was in a cottage on the Dulverton side of the bridge. This kept us going until we reached my Grandma's home at Grants Cottages just beyond the Roundhouse on the Minehead road.

When they first moved to Exebridge, Mr Radford and his wife lived at 3 Staghound Cottages, near the

Main: *Exmoor in snow, 1947.*
Inset: *The main road at Exebridge and the Fisheries in the snow, 1976/7.*

The house at the Fishery, c.1970s, and the hatchery at the Fishery, with Percy Wensley in trilby hat with two helpers.

Exebridge Fisheries, early 1920s.

Anchor Inn. Thelma remembers:

Inside the floor was made of large stone slabs – very convenient when the river Exe overflowed and flooded these cottages, as it often did in the winter. My mother told me that as a child she could remember her father sliding down a plank from the bedroom window into a horse drawn cart, to be taken to work.

Grants Cottage was a better house than Staghound, but still with no gas, no electricity, no coal and only wood logs for heating to cook and provide hot water for washing and cleaning.

She remembers waiting what seemed hours for the water to drip from the spring at the rear of the house:

Yet my grandmother took in washing for some of the local gentry. A man would arrive with a pony and trap bringing a large wicker laundry basket full of dirty white linen, mainly bedding, shirts etc and expect to return with the previous laundry washed and ironed. I can remember seeing on my Granny's huge scrubbed table, a stack of gent's stiff collars, beautifully glossy and white. If anything was not satisfactory or had the slightest crease, it was returned to be laundered again.

I spent many happy hours with the lady who lived in the roundhouse. I recall she had a dark oak settle which I loved sitting on by the wood fire. One day she and I walked to Dulverton and we were almost in the town, when we were startled by dogs barking. There, on top of the little bridge, was a beautiful stag trapped by a pack of hounds. The stag was 'crying' and that lived in my mind for many years.

She also recalls visits to the small chapel just beyond the roundhouse, which was 'built of wood with seating for about 30 people'. She continues:

My granny was the caretaker and I remember going with her every Saturday to clean and prepare the chapel for the Sunday services. A bunch of flowers was always picked from my granfer's garden and lovingly arranged in a vase to stand on the harmonium.

Ernest remembers that the cottages were served with water by a communal pump in a cobbled yard at the rear:

Granny would fetch water from a spring in the wall at the junction of Morebath Road and the main road. She put up a poster advertising lemonade made by Starkey Knight and Ford, which she sold to passing cyclists and walkers.

He also remembers watching a lady plucking ducks which had been delivered alive in crates, and watching a horse-drawn trailer with two huge trees brought down from Exmoor:

... the trailer was so long, it needed two or three turns to manoeuvre past the roundhouse. Later in the thirties a steam driven lorry was used. Blocks were sawn at the sawmills for railway track wedges and I often rode on the lorry taking them to Dulverton Station with Mr Utter or Mr Otter who was the driver. They were dumped on a huge pile of wedges awaiting transport by rail.

Above all, Thelma remembers the quiet and the stillness:

Waking each morning in my granny's bedroom, even with the windows wide open, it was so quiet that all I could hear were the lambs bleating in the field opposite.

The Little Exe divides Exebridge in half and it readily floods, cutting Exebridge off from Dulverton. All three children remember playing a game to stand on Exe Bridge with one foot in Devon and the other in Somerset.

Ellen Maund's memories of Exebridge began in 1954 when she went to the Fishery. She recalls that Devon children walked to school in Morebath, while Somerset children went to Brushford School:

At that time all the people who lived in Exebridge were local and many had been born there. Now we have only three locals – Hildah Pyke, Mary Baker and Billy Gunter.

The houses were all on the old Carnarvon Estate, but were sold off in 1929/30 for between £100 and £150. No. 3 sold for £110 and the entire fishery plus the business for £7,500.

The Pykes were a most colourful family. Their grandmother was a Wensley and though apparently never went to school and couldn't read or write, nevertheless she ran a large laundry. Pixton estate put up the laundry hut for her, plus a pump which pumped the water from the river. The irons were old-fashioned flat irons which were heated on the stove, some were very heavy and some were guttered for frills. Her son William was a great character too. He was an expert timber man and could have been wealthy but, unfortunately for his wife and family, tended to squander his money!

The former railway line from Exebridge to Brushford, K. Nelder with dog.

Bury Bridge, early 1900s.

Bury Football Club, 1946/47. Left to right, standing: *B. Cockram, W. Pollard, F. Patterson, R. Bryant, H. Goss;* sitting: *B. Stevens, A. Starks, T. Blackmore, S. Williams, J. Smith, L. Venn.*

SEVENTEEN
⚜
BURY

Bury – known as Brompton Bury until the late-eighteenth century – was divided from Dulverton and Exebridge in the 1840s by the Minehead and Dulverton toll-road. Prior to that, the division was created by the Little Exe, which joined its big brother, the Barle, at Exebridge. Mrs Mary Baker gave us this detailed description of Bury.

Lady Harriet's Drive – named after Lady Harriet Acland – runs from Pixton House across the road at Wier. On the left are the ruins or mounds of Bury Castle, a medieval fort guarding the entrance to the Carnarvon estates. The Drive enters Bury just above the church and school on the road into the village.

Coming into Bury from the other side of the village, Gilclose Farm is on the corner. At one time, some of the outer buildings there had village shops, including a butcher's. On the right there is a thatched cottage.

A little further on is the Methodist Chapel. Lord Carnarvon leased the plot for the building of the chapel in 1889. It was turned into a house in the late 1980s.

On the left, over the ridge past the old Reading Room, was the blacksmith's forge. The last blacksmith was Jack Thorne. A lovely three-span packhorse bridge crosses the river at the ford. On the further side of the bridge is a listed cottage, Cowlings. There is a Victorian postbox built into the wall.

To the left in the Square is Old School House. The first schoolmaster was Joseph Webber, who was later followed by the Greenhoughs. Bury School was built in 1890 and began to be used as an Anglican Chapel of Ease, which was turned into a house in 1980.

The road to the right follows Lady Harriet's Drive past Hunts Farm, up to the Lodge Gates and continues past two cottages at Clammer. A little further up the valley, a wide track leads to Lyncombe Lake and to the farm owned by Louisa Gate. Staying on the lower track beside the river, you come to Higher Lodge Gate at the hamlet of Hartford. The Lodge itself is by the gate.

Hartford Mill has a big water-wheel and, over the stream, there is still an old stone clapper bridge. Crossing the bridge, by a big stone, is Mutton Pie Well, with lovely pure water. The water from this well is supposed to guard against a great many complaints.

The highest point on Haddon Hill is called Hadborough. The Trig point is 355m high and close by are three Roman tumuli, where Roman coins were found.

Mrs Baker's grandmother lived at Wynn Farm and her grandfather worked for the Pixton estate. They had four daughters, all of whom went into service, one as a lady's maid to Mrs Shoppee at Hollam, travelling abroad with her, and Mary's mother went to the Exe Valley Fishery. Mary remembers going to school at Bury where there were only five pupils:

My mother paid two and sixpence a week for me to go there and she paid one and sixpence a week for me to have piano lessons at school. We were taught by Miss Greenhaugh. I used to go from school to have lunch with my gran at No. 2, Bury. I cycled to school each day from Exebridge.

Clearly, the attendance must have dropped considerably from 1889 when *Kelly's Directory* included reference to a (mixed) National school at Bury which was '... also used as a chapel of ease'. Details were given as follows: '.. it will hold 60 children, average attendance 44; and is supported in part by the Earl of Carnarvon; William Clark, master.'

An item in the *West Somerset Free Press* of 1901 reported that:

The children attending Sunday School in Bury had their annual treat to Brompton Regis. The party was conveyed by wagon trimmed with flags and evergreens and kindly lent by the Dowager Lady Carnarvon. All manner of games were freely indulged in before tea and a well contested game of cricket.

In 1918, J.W. Firth, the Diocesan Inspector, reported:

The teaching has been methodical and reverent, and the children have duly profited by it. Their answering was remarkably even and intelligent, and their clear and definite knowledge of the Catechism deserves special mention. The Repetition was perfectly known, and the written work was neat and almost entirely free from errors. A very good and useful year's work has been accomplished.

Edward VII Coronation Banner 'God Bless you both', Bidgood Cottage is the one with the with tall chimneys.

Patent medicine man at Bury. Note the 'Bliss Native Herbs'.

Curtis family wedding, early 1900s. Mrs Curtis senr is sitting by the bridesmaids.

The Curtis family at Bury.

Above left: *Bill Cording, the last known member of the farming family.*

Above: *Bill Thorne in uniform.*

Left: *The Curtis family. The young lady is the girl who married John Thorne in the late 1890s.*

Right: *W. Thorne, father to J. Thorne, both worked as blacksmiths.*

❧ *Bury* ❧
Folk

Far left: *John Thorne at Bury with a bull.*

Left: *Mr D. Hill at Hunts Farm, Bury, with his favourite bull Herbie.*

Right: *The Forge at Bury. Mr and Mrs Thorne are standing with young Bill with the motorcycle and sidecar.*

Below: *The wedding of John Thorne, possibly in the late 1890s.*

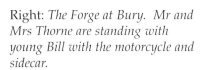

Scout camp, 1979.

Polish Scouts marching to church, 1978.

Main: *Fête at Bury, opened by Edward du Cann, early 1970s.*

Inset: *Edward du Cann and his daughters with their hosts and grandchild at Pine Cottage, Bury.* **Also in the picture from left to right:** *Shirley and Mrs Tout; and John and Blanche Baker of Gilclose Farm.*

Mrs Mollie Leadbetter gave us the following story told to her by Mrs Rene Davey, whose family farmed at Skilgate. Mrs Davey said the Master at Bury School was very strict and she didn't like him much:

Mrs Rene Davey and her two brothers attended Bury School around 1910. To get there, she and her younger brother shared a pony. They set off, one walking and the other riding the pony. The rider rode as fast as possible (pony willing!) to a half-way point, dismounted and tied the pony to a gate and walked the rest of the way to school. The walker found the pony, mounted and rode on to school. The pony was put into a nearby field until school was over, then the journey home was a repeat of the morning's efforts.

Mrs Mary Baker also recalls:

When my mum was a little girl, the Devon and Somerset Staghounds used to meet at Bury and if they killed the stag anywhere near, my mum used to hold the horses and the riders would give her tuppence while they went down to the water.

When my gran got old, my auntie gave up her job in service in London to look after gran. We used to visit them every Sunday at the Lodge. Once gran passed away, my aunt lived there alone... she kept chickens and one cock pheasant always lived in the run with the chickens. Auntie always used to get worried when the shoot started and always saw to it that he was left in the chicken run for safety.

When my aunt was sitting in her kitchen one day she saw Mr Auberon Herbert on his horse. 'Oh, Miss Medic, I've just come down Hartford Bottom – you know all the property round here belongs to me. As I was riding down the valley someone came along in a vehicle and shouted out of the window to me to "Get out

of the b....y way!" This upset me so much I'm going to padlock the gates at each end of the valley.' So it wasn't long before they brought the padlock and keys and locked both gates. He gave auntie the keys to open the gate for anyone who had to go up the valley and after a while they gave some keys to the two cottages at Clammer.

Locals of Bury included the Curtis and Thorne families (which were linked by marriage), Major Eustance and Mrs Maria Poles (sister to Rodney Peake of Dulverton Laundry). The Major was a very keen angler and teacher of fly-fishing and Eustace was also a well-known falconer.

For several years in the 1970s and '80s, when Mr Hill was at Hunts Farm, the Polish Scouts camped each year beside the Haddeo – the Boy Scouts one year, the Girl Scouts the next. The Polish connection came about through Aubrey Herbert of Pixton and his wartime association with the Polish Army.

Bury School certificate of merit, 1891.

As it was before work began at the Heritage Centre.

Another view of the wreck.

EIGHTEEN

❧❦❧

THE HERITAGE & EXHIBITION CENTRE

We hope (though it is difficult to be certain) that the Heritage Centre occupies the site of Dulverton's ancient Guildhall. When writing of this Centre, one must first write of the Dulverton and District Civic Society which was formed in January 1989. This evolved from a studies course offered by Bristol University entitled 'Developing your Community – an informal course for people interested in the future of their community' (no educational qualification needed), which was held in Dulverton in 1986. The aim was to preserve the quiet character of this very small rural town and help it to survive against the odds of its becoming a soulless dormitory.

Dulverton has always had a beautiful setting on the edge of Exmoor. It has a great deal to offer, with relaxed and friendly people, and a great tradition of farming behind it. A Heritage Centre seemed a good way to preserve the way of life of people past and present, for future generations – somewhere for locals as well as visitors to come, enjoy and perhaps learn.

In 1988, the building to the rear of the Dulverton Ironmongers came on the market. It was an interesting place as it had, some 200 years earlier, formed the stables, malthouse, courtyard and outbuildings to the seventeenth-century inn called the Lamb. By the late-nineteenth century, it had in part become Germans Ironmongers, with the malthouse and outbuildings converted to four small cottages. In the latter part of the twentieth century, these again became storage places as the people were re-housed. In the middle was the open courtyard. Visitors looking for an old or obscure fitting were told 'if it's not there, look in the attic' (this was up very ancient and rickety stairs) and, if still not found, 'go across the yard at the back – it might be in one of those' (meaning the old cottages). This meant picking one's way through knee-high nettles and weeds. Those were the days!

These were the buildings chosen for the Heritage

Florence Locke and parents outside what would later become the Heritage Centre.

Centre. As a result, the Dulverton and District Civic Society was formed in 1989 and promptly set about raising money in order to purchase the site and develop their ideas. Through the generosity of the Dulverton Trust, set up by Gilbert Wills, Lord Dulverton, the buildings were acquired. However, a great deal of fund-raising had to follow if the Heritage and Exhibition Centre was to become reality.

As funds accumulated, so work began and as it progressed, the Centre gradually opened, one gallery at a time, with the exhibition gallery one of the first, holding an early spring exhibition for Dulverton Art Group in 1992.

In 1995, a modern library and the Exmoor National Park Visitor Centre took the place of the old German Ironmongers which are linked with the Heritage Centre so that visitors can pass from one to the other.

Within the Centre is a Victorian cottage, known as Granny Baker's – one of the original four. Exhibits in the main entrance, gallery and other rooms are changed or renewed and updated each year. The Centre tries to create a new exhibition each year in the photographic gallery, which houses the Exmoor photographic archive, as well as interesting visual displays. The number of visitors each year averages 20,000.

The biggest ongoing project at the time of writing is the building of the model of Dulverton Station. It is housed in the old barn to the rear or front of the Centre (depending on which way the building is entered!). This barn, known locally as the Cheese Store, is very old and oddly shaped. A small garden borders the area, which contains a pebble mosaic created by children from Dulverton Middle School in 1998. Close by is a seat dedicated to a member of the German family who lived in one of the cottages.

The Heritage Centre survives because of its volunteers who are generous with their time – and also thanks to the donations from our visitors.

Top: *Outside the Heritage Centre.*

Above: *Musical evening at Pixton, June 1990 –
Steven Pugsley, Chairman of Dulverton and
District Civic Society, helping to raise funds for
the Heritage Centre.*

Right: *Heritage Centre Courtyard.*

Above: *Heritage Centre art gallery.*

Right: *Ground-floor display, Heritage Centre, 1997.*

Below left: *Granny Baker's kitchen.*

Below right: *A copy of a drawing of the premises before the Heritage Centre evolved, by Revd Donald Flatt.*

Lower Baronsdown Lodge after a major restructure, during which the thatched roof was removed, an upper floor put in and the roof slated, c.1920s. The building was pulled down after the Second World War, around 1947.

The Mount, showing Rose Cottage in the centre and Horner Cottage above to the right, before 1911.

Snippets or Last Thoughts

In 1719, a William Balmont held the lease of Bilbao House. He died in South Molton Prison. (We have no idea why he was incarcerated, or the circumstances of his death.) In a local bible the following was found, an entry for 13 August 1820:

My father James Balmont was taken ill and died 19th August 1820, aged 73 years. Buried August 27th at six o'clock in the evening on a Sunday. His coffin was made by Robert Fisher at the cost of £1.15s.0d. His bearers were: John & Robert Fisher, John & William Balmont, Richard and William Grant.

Guildhall Terrace – a row of three houses – was built in 1900 to repay a debt by Fishers to Germans.

An item in the *West Somerset Free Press* of 1901 read:

A Spanish coin from 1600 was discovered in debris at Dulverton. It was not known how the coin came to rest in West Somerset but it was found by a man building a wall.

Monmouth Terrace was owned by Robert Warren between 1813 and 1887. A miller, he also owned Town Mills and houses. He was Jack Warren's grandfather.

G.R. Quaife researched social history and behaviour in the seventeenth century in Somerset (1601–1660). His research was based on depositions presented to the Quarter Sessions of Somerset and the Consistory Court of the Diocese of Bath & Wells – a most fascinating book. Within it was a paragraph or two that really set Dulverton and its surrounding area into history:

Lucy Francis and Mary Hodges were two women who did the circuit of Inns and Alehouses with some success, especially in Dulverton and Exebridge. The girls worked in pairs and while Lucy was in a room at an inn with the door locked and windows barred, Mary was in the next chamber with another man.

Lucy recalled a major error which cost her 2s.6d. While at a Dulverton Inn a gentleman had offered her 2s.6d. to have the use of her body – but she demanded 3s. – the poor man had but 2s.6d. and if she had known he had no more she would have dealt for the same. She explained that 'by that means I lost a good bargain'.

They worked hard for their 'bargains', visiting weavers at their homes, or in the shops where some of them worked. If caught or confessed, punishment could be the stocks for a while, a whipping, or – dare one suggest – 'payment in kind'.

Judge Jeffreys sentenced at least six men of Dulverton to be executed. Of these, three were later pardoned – one of them was a Peppin (much money must have changed hands!). Of the other three, one died of smallpox before execution, but the other two were executed in Dulverton, Judge Jeffreys having decreed that execution must take place in the home town of the convicted person. Humphrey Sydenham was the lord of the manor at the time and disliked unnecessary cruelty, so as soon as the executioners had departed, the head and quarters of the executed men were removed from the bridges and gates and decently buried.

Gilbert Wills, when elevated to the peerage in 1926, chose the title of Dulverton because of his happy childhood here. It was he who formed the Dulverton Trust.

The grandson of Arthur Puttock of Dulverton – Philip Gammon – has been principal pianist for the Royal Ballet since 1999, having joined them as a very young man in 1964. His father was born and grew up here, until lack of work forced him to move.

A Dulverton "At Home"

Meet in Fore Street, Dulverton, between 1900 and 1910.

Meet in Dulverton, opposite Ellertons, c.1918.

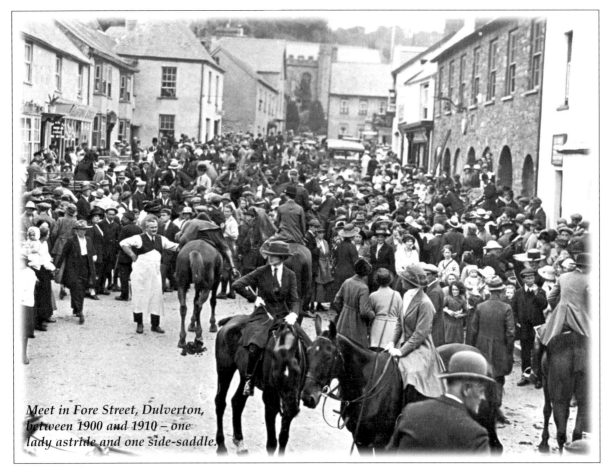

Meet in Fore Street, Dulverton, between 1900 and 1910 – one lady astride and one side-saddle.

A gathering in Dulverton, c.1902, with one lady riding side-saddle.

Carnarvon Arms and station.

Snow scene looking from The Cottage to the Workhouse (to the right) and an iced-up river, 1940s.

George Barrell's shop, Dulverton, 1945.

The same view, c.1925/6, when the shop belonged to T. Lock, saddler.

Fore Street, Dulverton, a view taken from the Town Hall steps in 1945.

Fore Street in 1974 – Jack's cows returning to the field after milking.

The White Hart in 1953 as the Golden Guernsey Milk Bar.

Thorne Bros and the Lamb Hotel, c.1930.

Exmoor House in 1962, showing the single-track carriageway.

Exmoor House in 1964 showing the widened carriageway and car-parking.

A JUBILEE YEAR UPDATE

The reprint of *The Book of Dulverton* has enabled us to include details of events in Dulverton since the turn of the century.

Golden Jubilee and Recreation Ground Refurbishment

The Queen's Golden Jubilee Celebrations were held on 3 June 2002. With Fore Street closed, the entertainment went on all day with dancing, a tea party, live music and a pig roast.

The celebrations were arranged on the basis that any surplus on the Jubilee Day fundraising events were to go towards the refurbishment of the Recreation Ground in Pound Walk.

Following on from the Jubilee there was further fundraising, including a sponsored walk of about 52 miles up and down the Exe and Barle valleys by local firemen and families which raised about £1700.

Grants were obtained from various funds, including £25000 from Barclays Bank with the proviso that local school children should plan the new 'rec' and have a say on what equipment was to be purchased. There was a Grand Opening of the refurbished Recreation Ground in September 2003.

Dulverton firemen who did the sponsored walk in aid of the Recreational Ground Refurbishment Left to right: Tom Buckingham, Rick Stanbury and Jon Snell.

Vikki Nuttall

Above and below: *The Golden Jubilee, 2002.*

The opening of the refurbished Recreational Ground, September 2003.

Exmoor Oral History

The Dulverton and District Civic Society were involved in supporting Birdie Johnson in creating the Exmoor Oral History Archive which was completed in 2001.

Birdie recorded interviews with over 40 people from across Exmoor providing a unique opportunity to record the memories of those who live and work on Exmoor.

The recordings are now available at the Somerset Records Office (or on line at http//www.somerset.gov.uk/archives) whilst the supporting book *Reflections – Life Portraits of Exmoor* is available to be purchased at the Heritage Centre.

Yellow Lines

On pages 99 and 101 you will have read about the advent of car parks in Dulverton but the Guildhall development didn't come on its own in that 'yellow lines' arrived as it was felt they were necessary to ensure that motorists used the car parks – and paid for their use.

Dulverton Town Hall

It is reported earlier in the book that extensive renovations had been carried out in 1999 and 2000. After five years of fund raising and building, the new extension of the Town Hall was officially re-opened in June 2001 by the Lord Lieutenant of Somerset, Lady Gass.

The Town Hall had been completely refurbished at a cost of £140,000. The ground floor now consists of a foyer area, suitable for committee meetings, exhibitions or as a 'sale area' for local organisations. The new extension includes toilets, a kitchen, internal stairs and a lift to the main hall on the first floor.

Bolving

In October 2003 the regulars at the Rock Inn decided to hold a Bolving Competition and this has now become an annual event for charity.

Bolving is mimicking the sound a red deer stag makes (otherwise known as roaring or belling) during the deer rutting season.

Those who are able to obtain an 'answer' from an actual stag are judged for performance by a panel of 'experts'.

The competition gained national recognition when local photographer and presenter Johnny Kingdom came along to judge the competition and included the event in his TV documentary *A Year on Exmoor Series 2* on BBC Television.

Dulverton by Starlight

Just over ten years ago Jools Abbott and Rod Strutt, with the help of funding from a Leader project, launched what has become Dulverton by Starlight.

The Leader funding was matched by the local traders which enabled Christmas tree holders, lights and decorations to be purchased and put up in the town to provide a festive sight for local people and visitors to enjoy throughout the Christmas period.

Over the years this idea has been developed with now a specific day, the first Sunday in December, providing extended opening hours, an exhibition of nativity scenes, hand bell ringers, Santa's Grotto, Morris dancing, carol singing, complimentary drinks and seasonal snacks from the traders, a bazaar and a stunning firework display to round off the day.

Broadband

BT activated the Dulverton exchange on 16 February 2005 enabling businesses and households to access broadband internet with connection speeds from 256 Kbps to 2 Mbps.

The War Memorial

Although Miss B K Abbott at the Cottage donated the Recreational Field to the town in 1920 in memory of the Dulvertonians lost in the First World War and those lost in the two World Wars are listed in the church it was not until 2006 when the local branch of the Royal British Legion organised a public collection that a suitable memorial was erected.

The memorial designed and crafted by local stone carver, Laurence Beckford, was unveiled by Major General Dare Wilson CBE MC DL FRG.

Dulverton War Memorial.

Those commemorated are:

First World War

Ernest Baker (Castle Court), John Bristow (Higher Broford), Cecil Burnett (Lady Street), Edwin Chilcott (Castle Court), Robert Collyns (The Green), Charles Cording (Fore Street), Walter Court (Hawkridge), Archibald Farrier (Battleton), Frank Floyd (Perry Cottages), George Fyfe (Fore Street), James Giles (Lady Street), Sidney Goss (Battleton), James Gunney (Carnarvon Arms Cottages), William Hawkins (Highercombe Cottages), George Hobbs (High Street), Frank Johnson (no details), Albert Kingdon (Barns Close), George Lugg (Rosemary Lane), Fred Milton (Lyncombe Farm, Brompton Regis), Edward Murphy (no details), Fred Parkhouse (White Horse Inn), Sidney Roberts (Hawkwell Cottage), Herbert Rudd (High Street), John Sanger (Oldways End), Humphrey Sydenham (Battleton House), Isaac Saunders (Fore Street), John Tarr (New Inn), Cecil Tee (Rosemary Lane), Edward White (no details) and Francis Williams (Castle Court).

Second World War

Henry Chapman (West Hele, Jury), Roy Chilcott (Milhams Lane), Gilbert Farmer (Battleton), Albert Herniman (no details), John McFadzean (High Street), Walter Saunders (The Castle) and Clarence Stone (no details).

It also commemorates those lost on the sinking of HMS Dulverton in 1943.

*The Heritage Centre Dulverton Station
model railway, 1936.*

Heritage Centre Railway

Earlier in the book you will have read about Dulverton Station at Brushford and with the vision and forethought of some very dedicated volunteers, financial backing and provision of a dedicated home in the Cheese Store (now the Railway Shed) the dream of creating a Dulverton Station model railway 1936 has been realised.

The project is being continually developed but the model railway has been on view to members of the public on a regular basis.

In addition, from time to time the Heritage Centre also hosts in the Gallery an exhibition of Dulverton Station from 1866 to 1966 showing many photographs and railway memorabilia.

Sports Pavilion

In 2006, after eleven years of fund raising and planning, the Dulverton Sportsfield Charity completed a new pavilion and car park.

The pavilion, run by the Dulverton Sports and Social Club, provides a new home for the Dulverton Football, Cricket, Tennis and Squash Clubs, has a social room, kitchen and bar.

Secret Gardens

In August 2008 a group of people were persuaded to open their gardens to the public for one Sunday to raise funds for charity. This has become an annual event with more gardens both old and new becoming available each year.

The event gives a rare opportunity for people to see gardens which are normally hidden behind walls or houses. The gardens suit all tastes, from those who like plants and shrubs giving all round colour, to those who love the impact of bedding plants. The gardens are of all shapes and sizes and stages of development, some being established for hundreds of years and others only recently started.

Tour of Britain

On 17 September 2009 the Tour of Britain cycle race passed through Dulverton. It was the sixth stage from Frome to Bideford, some 184 kms.

Several roads in and around Dulverton were closed for a short time and although there was a small crowd in Dulverton there were a lot more people taking advantage of the sunny weather and watching the cyclists on Winsford Hill.

Dulverton Films

Dulverton Town Hall had not had regular film showings for more than half a century, apart from when a film society was set up for a brief spell in the 1970s, but in 2010 this changed.

The Town Hall Management Committee worked with Victoria Thomas from Withypool, who had completed a similar project in Minehead, to establish Dulverton Films.

They obtained significant funding and assistance from local organisations which enabled modern equipment to be purchased.

Dulverton Films show up to two films a month, one of which, of course, has been the locally filmed *Land Girls*.

Mayor

At the Dulverton Town Council's Annual General Meeting in May 2011 it was agreed that instead of having a Chairman they should be a Mayor and Chris Nelder was duly elected.

*The Mayor,
Chris Nelder.*

Stargazing

In November 2011 Exmoor was granted International Dark-Sky Reserve status and then in January 2012 Dulverton were asked to be part of BBC's *Stargazing Live* by turning off all of the lights at 8 o'clock.

The BBC were in the area for several days and interviewed a number of local people some of whom appeared live on the programme. Unfortunately after clear evenings earlier in the week the actual 'night' turned out to be overcast and wet and very little stargazing was possible.

Churchyard

It may be that not everybody was in agreement but the Dulverton Churchyard Committee Development Group, made up of members of the Dulverton PCC, Dulverton Town Council and members of the public, secured £50000 from 'Community Spaces' to create a wild life garden in the churchyard and improve the access to encourage local people to use the facility.

It was officially launched in July 2010 by botanist David Bellamy who announced he was opening 'God's Garden'.

Diamond Jubilee

The Diamond Jubilee celebrations in Dulverton and Brushford were spread over the extended weekend of 2 June to 5 June 2012 and although there was some rain all the events were very successful.

In Dulverton the Folk Festival was around all weekend with numerous events in the Town Hall and around the Town. On the Saturday the Heritage Centre had a fête on the area in front of the Guildhall Centre with spinning and weaving demonstrations, Exmoor Horn Sheep, the model railway, Morris dancing, lots of stalls and a BBQ.

On the Sunday there was a Civic Service at All Saints church, the unveiling of the Jubilee Oak and a picnic and games. This was followed by the Cricket Club's Duck Derby and other games on Exmoor Lawns.

The events continued on to the Monday with a Jubilee Fun Day at the Sportsfield which provided fun for all ages with competitions, games and races, the highlight being the traditional Jubilee tea party to round off the celebrations.

Brushford had a Fun Day at the Polo Field on the Saturday with a dog show, tug of war, games and races and a disco at the Parish Hall in the evening.
On the Sunday there was a Flower Festival and Thanksgiving service in the church followed on the Monday by a hog roast at Three Acres and the lighting of the beacon at Hulvaton Hill.

The celebrations were completed on the Tuesday by a street party in the centre of village with fancy dress and a traditional tea and then a barn dance in the Parish Hall in the evening.

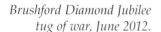

Brushford Diamond Jubilee tug of war, June 2012.

Dulverton Diamond Jubilee Sportsfield tea, June 2012.